Charles F. Taylor

Official Formulae of American Hospitals

Second Edition

Charles F. Taylor

Official Formulae of American Hospitals
Second Edition

ISBN/EAN: 9783337163204

Printed in Europe, USA, Canada, Australia, Japan

Cover: Foto ©Andreas Hilbeck / pixelio.de

More available books at **www.hansebooks.com**

OFFICIAL FORMULÆ.

—OF—

American Hospitals.

COLLECTED AND ARRANGED

—BY—

C. F. TAYLOR, M.D.,

EDITOR OF

THE MEDICAL WORLD.

Second Edition, Enlarged.

PUBLISHED BY
"THE MEDICAL WORLD,"
1520–1522 CHESTNUT STREET,
PHILADELPHIA.

GEO. F. LASHER, PRINT, PHILA.

Introduction to the First Edition.

I N collecting the matter for this book, all the principal, and nearly all the minor Hospitals in the United States were either visited or communicated with. Some hospitals have a printed list of formulæ; others have a few standard prescriptions, and still others have no established formulæ at all. The printed lists, the established prescriptions from those hospitals not having printed lists, and all other information of value, have been collected and are here presented. Omitting the lists of two or three hospitals that replied (strangely) "Not for publication," the writer feels that this collection is quite as complete as can well be made.

It is scarcely necessary to state that these formulæ do not represent the entirety of hospital practice. Certain mixtures being found useful in a large number of cases, they are prepared in large quantities to facilitate dispensing. This is important where a large number of cases are treated daily. Special cases, or cases presenting unusual indications, are treated according to indications presented. The writer has no admiration for doctors who blindly follow printed formulæ, and it is farthest from his desire that this book should encourage this large class of practitioners. The benefit intended is to place before the profession the remedies and combinations of remedies found most useful in our hospitals. The study of these cannot fail to give many hints and suggestions useful in private practice. It is hoped that the unlocking of these store-houses of experience will be considered a service to the profession.

C. F. TAYLOR.

PHILADELPHIA, August, 1885.

Introduction to the Second Edition.

T HE writer is highly gratified to see that the first edition of this book is so soon exhausted, and that another is called for. It has been suggested that an index be added; but when it is noticed that the table of contents may serve as an index to the hospitals, and that most of the hospitals have their formulæ divided into departments, such as liniments, pills, mixtures, etc., it will be seen that further indexing is quite unnecessary. It has been remarked by a few that the directions and indications for the use of each formula are generally not given. It has been our aim to present the different pharmacopœias just exactly as they exist in the different hospitals, without assuming the responsibility of adding, substracting or changing a single word. We will say that it is presumed that each hospital physician can safely rely upon his knowledge of pathology and therapeutics for the intelligent use of a formula; it is hoped that the same presumption may as safely be extended to the average private practitioner.

C. F. TAYLOR.

PHILADELPHIA, April, 1886.

CONTENTS.

PHARMACOPŒIA

OF THE

Hospital of the University of Pennsylvania.

COLLYRIA.

℞ Atropiæ sulphatis...................... gr. iv
   Aquæ destillatæ........................ f℥ j
   M.

℞ Duboisiæ sulphatis.................... gr. ¼
   Aquæ destillatæ........................ f℥ j
   M.

℞ Eserinæ................................ gr. ij
   Aquæ destillatæ........................ f℥ j
   M.

℞ Zinci sulphatis....................... gr. iv
   Aquæ destillatæ........................ f℥ j
   M.

℞ Aluminis .... gr. ij
   Aquæ destillatæ........................ f℥ j
   M.

℞ Acidi gallici............................ ʒ i,
   Glycerinæ .... f ʒ j

M.

℞ Acidi tannici............................ ʒ ij
   Glycerinæ................................ f ʒ j

M.

℞ Pilocarpiæ nitratis .... gr. ij
   Aquæ destillatæ...................... f ʒ j

M.

— o —

GARGARISMATA.

Gargarisma Composita.

℞ Potassii chloratis....................... ʒ ij
   Rhois glabri............................ ʒ j

M.—Sig. Put in a pint of boiling water and simmer to ⅔ pint in an earthen vessel, and then strain.

— o —

GLYCERITA.

Glyceritum Plumbi Subacetatis.

℞ Plumbi acetatis........................ Ɗ v
   Plumbi oxidi............................ ʒ j
   Glycerinæ .... ʒ vij

Heat for half an hour in a boiling glycerine bath, constantly stirring, and filter in a heated condition.

LINIMENTA.

1.—Linimentum Tiglii.

℞ Ol. tiglii.................................... f ℥ j
   Ol. olivæ.................................... f ℥ vij
  M.

2.—Linimentum Chloroformi Compositum.

℞ Chloroformi.............................. f ℥ ij
   Tr. aconiti radicis....................... f ℥ ss
   Aquæ ammoniæ......................... f ℥ ss
   Ol. olivæ.................................. f ℥ v
  M.

3.—Linimentum Iodinii Compositum.

℞ Chloroformi.............................. f ℥ ij
   Tr. iodinii................................. f ℥ vj
  M.

LIQUORES.

1.—Liquor Picis Alkalinus.

℞ Picis liquidæ....................... ..... f ℥ ij
   Potassæ................................... ℥ j
   Aquæ...................................... f ℥ v
  M.—Sig. One teaspoonful to four or eight tablespoon-
fuls of water; for external use.

2.—Liquor Chloralis.

℞ Chloralis hydratis...................... gr. lxxx
   Aquæ...................................... f ℥ j
  M.—Dose, one to two teaspoonfuls.

LOTIONES.

1.—Lotio Nigra.

℞　Hydrargyri chloridi mitis.............　gr. iij
　　Liq. calcis............................　f ℥ j
　M.

2.—Lotio Plumbi Acetatis et Opii.

℞　Plumbi acetatis........................　gr. x
　　Tr. opii................................　f ʒ j ss
　　Aquæ..................................　f ʒ vj ss
　M.

---o---

MISTURÆ.

1.—Mistura Ferri Arsenicalis.

℞　Vini ferri..............................　f ʒ iij
　　Liq. potassii arsenitis.................　f ʒ ss
　　Syrupi.................................　f ʒ j ss
　　Aquæ..................................　f ʒ iij
　M.—Dose, one teaspoonful, diluted, after meals.

2.—Mistura Acida Astringens.

℞　Acidi sulphurici aromatici...........　♏ xl
　　Ext. hematoxyli......................　ʒ j
　　Tr. opii camphoratæ..................　f ʒ iv
　　Syrupi zingiberis.....................　f ʒ iv
　M.—Dose, two teaspoonfuls.

3.—Mistura Cretæ Composita.

℟ Mist. cretæ............................... f℥ v
Tr. catechu.............................
Tr. opii camphoratæ............āā... f℥ j ss
M.—Dose, a teaspoonful.

4.—Mistura Olei Phosphorati.

℞ Ol. phosphorati......................... ℳ xvj
Ol. gaultheriæ.................. .... ℳ viij
Muc. acaciæ............................ f℥ j
M.—Dose, one to two teaspoonfuls.

5.—Mistura Potassii Chloratis et Ferri.

℞ Potassii chloratis....................... ℨ ss
Tr. ferri chloridi...................... f℥ j
Aquæ.................................... f℥ vij
M.—Dose, one teaspoonful.

6.—Mistura Ferri Acetata.

℞ Tr. ferri chloridi....................... ℳ xx
Acidi acetici diluti.................... ℳ xx
Syrupi.................................... ℨ ij
Liq. ammonii acetatis................ f℥ vij
M.— Dose, two to four teaspoonfuls.

7.—Mistura Ferri Acida.

℞ Ferri sulphatis......................... gr. ij
Magnesii sulphatis..................... ℨ j ss
Acidi sulphurici diluti................ ℳ xv
Infusi quassiæ........................... f℥ j
M.—Dose, a tablespoonful.

8.—Mistura Ferri Aperiens.

℞   Ferri sulphatis............................   gr. ij
     Magnesii sulphatis.....................   ℥ ij
     Aquæ......................................   f ℥ j
     M.—Dose, a tablespoonful.

9.—Mistura Potassii Iodidi Fortior.

℞   Potassii iodidi...........................   ℥ ss
     Aquæ cinnamomi.......................   f ℥ j
     M.—A teaspoonful equal to 30 grs. of iodide of potassium.

10.—Mistura Potassii Iodidi.

℞   Potassii iodidi...........................   gr. xl
     Aquæ cinnamomi.......................   f ℥ j
     M.—Dose, one or two teaspoonfuls.

11.—Mistura Potassii Iodidi Composita.

℞   Potassii iodidi...........................   gr. xx
     Hydrargyri chloridi corrosivi.........   gr. 1-6
     Aquæ cinnamomi.......................   f ℥ j
     M.—Dose, two to four teaspoonfuls.

12.—Mistura Hydrargyri Composita.

℞   Hydrargyri chloridi corrosivi.........   gr, ⅓
     Potassii iodidi...........................   gr. lxxx
     Aquæ menthæ piperitæ...............   f ℥ j
     M.—S.   Dose, one to two teaspoonfuls.

13.—Mistura Giberti.

℞   Hydrargyri iodidi rubri............,......   gr. ⅓
     Potassii iodidi..........................   gr. xvj
     Aquæ...   f ʒ j
Solve et adde—
     Syrupi simplicis..........................   f ʒ vij
M.—Dose, a tablespoonful.

14.—Mistura Hydrargyri et Ferri.

℞   Hydrargyri chloridi corrosivi.........   gr. iv
     Tr. ferri chloridi.......................   f ʒ j
M.—Dose, ten drops.

15.—Mistura Potassii Bromidi.

℞   Potassii bromidi ....   ʒ ij, gr. xl
     Aquæ cinnamomi........................   f ʒ j
M.—Dose, one to two teaspoonfuls.

16.—Mistura Sodii Composita.

℞   Sodii bicarbonatis.......................   gr. xx
     Acidi carbolici...........................   gtt. ij
     Acaciæ....................................
     Sacchari...................,.....ā ā...   q. s.
     Spts. lavandulæ comp.................   f ʒ ij
     Aquæ ....   f ʒ vj
M.—Dose, a teaspoonful two hours after meals.

17.—Mistura Olei Morrhuæ Composita.

℞   Ol morrhuæ..........................   f ʒ j
     Tr. iodinii comp.......................   ℳ viij
M.—Dose, one to four teaspoonfuls.

18.—Mistura Olei Morrhuæ et Ætheris.

℞   Mist. ol. morrhuæ..................... f ℨ j
    Ætheris .... ℳ xvj
    M.—Dose, one to four teaspoonfuls.

19.—Mistura Olei Morrhuæ et Calcis Lacto-Phosphatis.

℞   Ol. morrhuæ ....
    Mucil. acaciæ....................āā... f ℨ ij
    Fiat emulsio et adde—
    Syr. calcis lacto-phosphatis........... f ℥ ss

20.—Mistura Hyoscyami et Morphiæ.

℞   Morphiæ acetatis...................... gr. ¼
    Tr. hyoscyami......................... f ℨ j ss
    Syr. tolutanæ.......................... f ℨ ij ss
    Aquæ..................................... f ℨ ss
    M.—Dose, two teaspoonfuls.

21.—Mistura Ammonii Chloridi.

℞   Ammonii chloridi..................... gr. xx
    Syr. scillæ............................. f ℨ ij
    Mist. glycyrrhizæ comp............... f ℨ vj
    M.—Dose, two to four teaspoonfuls.

22.—Mistura Cinchoniæ Acida.

℞   Cinchoniæ sulphatis................... gr. xij
    Acidi nitromuriatici dil................ f ℨ ss
    Aquæ cinnamomi...................... f ℨ vij ss
    Ft. sol. Dose, two teaspoonfuls in water, before meals.

23.—Mistura Guaiaci Composita.

℞ Pulv. resinæ guaiaci......................
Potassii iodidi.....................āā... gr. x
Vini colchici seminis.................. f ℨ ss
Aquæ cinnamomi........................
Syrupi ....āā... f ℨ iv
M.—Dose, a tablespoonful.

24.—Mistura Gentianæ Acida.

℞ Acidi nitromuriatici dil................ ℳ xl
Inf. gentianæ comp...............ad... f ℥ j
M.—Dose, two teaspoonfuls.

25.—Mistura Arsenicalis.

℞ Liq. potassii arsenitis.................. f ℨ ss
Tr. quassiæ............................. f ℨ ij
Syrupi..................................... f ℨ v ss
M.—Dose, one teaspoonful, diluted, immediately after meals.

26.—Mistura Ætheris Composita.

℞ Spt. æther. comp...................... f ℨ ij ss
Tr. iobeliæ............................... f ℨ ss
Aquæ camphoræ....................... f ℨ v
M.—Dose, one to two teaspoonfuls.

27.—Mistura Cinchoniæ Sulphatis.

℞ Cinchoniæ sulphatis................... gr. xxiv
Acidi sulphurici dil.................... ℳ xxv
Aquæ menthæ piperitæ.........ad... f ℥ j
Ft. sol.   Dose, one to two teaspoonfuls.

28.—Mistura Deweesii.

℞ Tr. guaiaci comp........................... f℥ vj
    Tr. cantharidis........................... f℥ ss
    Tr. aloes................................. f℥ ij
    Tr. ferri chloridi........................ f℥ ij
    M.—Sig. Two to four teaspoonfuls, three times a day.

29.—Mistura Olei Ricini.

℞ Ol. ricini.............. ....
    Glycerinæ ....āā... f℥ j
    Ol. menthæ piperitæ.............. .... gtt. iij
    M.

30.—Mistura Olei Morrhuæ Composita.

℞ Ol. morrhuæ.............................
    Extract. malti ....āā... ℥ ss
    M.

31.—Mistura Croton-Chloralis.

℞ Croton-chloralis hydratis............... gr. x
    Syrupi.............................. f℥ ij
    Aquæ.................................... f℥ vj
    M.—Sig. Two teaspoonfuls, or a tablespoonful, every
four hours.

—o—

PILULÆ.

1.—Pilula Opii et Plumbi.

℞ Pulv. opii............................... gr. ⅓
    Plumbi acetatis.......................... gr. ij
    M. et ft. pil. No. 1.

2.—Pilula Opii et Acidi Tannici.

℞ Pulv. opii.. gr. ⅓
Acidi tannici............................... gr. iij
M. et ft. pil. No. 1.

3.—Pilula Hydrargyri Iodidi Viridi.

℞ Hydrargyri iodidi viridi............... gr. ¼
Confectionis rosæ....................... gr. ij
M. et ft. pil. No. 1.

4.—Pilula Colocynthidis Composita.

℞ Ext. colocynthidis comp............... gr. ij
Ext. belladonnæ........................... gr. ⅓
Ext. gentianæ...................... ...... gr. j
Ol. carui...................................... gtt. ss
M. et ft. pil. No. 1.

5.—Pilula Podophylli Composita.

℞ Resinæ podophylli....................... gr. 1-6
Pulv. rhei................................... gr. ij
Ext. belladonnæ.................... .... gr. ¼
Ol. carui.................................... gtt. ss
M. et ft. pil. No. 1.

6.—Pilula Cinchoniæ Composita.

℞ Cinchoniæ sulphatis.................... gr. j ss
Acidi arseniosi............................ gr. 1-35
Strychniæ sulphatis..................... gr. 1-35
M. et ft. pil. No. 1.

7.—Pilula Arsenicalis Composita.

℞ Acidi arseniosi............................ gr. 1-35
    Cinchoniæ sulphatis.................... gr. j ss
    Ferri et potassii tartratis.............. gr. ij
  M. et ſt. pil. No. 1.

8.—Pilula Cinchoniæ cum Ferro.

℞ Cinchoniæ sulphatis.................... gr. ij
    Pulv. ferri................................ gr. j
    Strychniæ................................ gr. 1-30
  M. et ſt. pil. No. 1.

9.—Pilula Argenti Nitratis.

℞ Argenti nitratis......................... gr. ¼
    Pulv. opii................................ gr. 1-12
  M. et ſt. pil. No. 1.

10.—Pilula Ferri Composita.

℞ Acidi arseniosi......................... gr. 1-35
    Strychniæ sulphatis.................. gr. 1-35
    Ext. belladonnæ...................... gr. 1-5
    Cinchoniæ sulphatis................. gr. j ss
    Pil. ferri carbonatis.................. gr. ij ss
  M. et ſt. pil. No. 1.

11.—Pilula Arsenicalis.

℞ Acidi arseniosi......................... gr. 1-20
    Confectionis rosæ..................... gr. ij
  M. et ſt. pil. No. 1.

12. –Pilula Auri et Sodii Chloridi.

℞   Auri et sodii chloridi.................   g ⅛
      Tragacanthæ ....   gr. j ss
      Sacchari.................................   q. s.
M. et ft. pil. No. 1. One twice a day after meals.

13.—Pilula Camphoræ Monobromidi.

℞   Camphoræ monobromidi..............   gr. ij ss
      Confectionis rosæ......................   q. s.
M. et ft. pil. No. 1.—Sig. One or two, every two hours as directed.

—o—

PULVERES.

1.—Pulvis Bismuthi Compositus.

℞   Bismuthi subnitratis....................   gr. x
      Pepsinæ ....
      Pulv. aromatici...............āā...   gr. v
M. et ft. chart. No. 1.

2.—Pulvis Sodæ Compositus.

℞   Sodii bicarbonatis......................
      Pulv. zingiberis........................
      Pulv. calumbæ...............āā...   gr. ij ss
M. et ft. chart. No. 1.

3.—Pulvis Bismuthi.

℞   Bismuthi subnitratis............ ....   gr. xv
Ft. chart. No. 1.

4.—Pulvis Santonini.

℞   Santonini ....   gr. ¼
       Sacchari.....................................   gr. ij
Ft. chart. No. 1.

5.—Pulvis Rhei Compositus.

℞   Pulv. rhei...................................   gr. iij
       Sodii bicarbonatis.......................   gr. x
       Pulv. zingiberis...........................   gr. ij
M. et ft. chart. No. 1.

6.—Pulvis Buchu Compositus.

℞   Buchu......................................   ℥ j
       Sodii bicarbonatis.......................   ʒ iij
       Folii belladonnæ.........................   gr. viij
M. et ft. chart. No. 1.   Sig.   Put in a pint of boiling water, and when cold, strain; dose, a wineglassful three times a day.

7.—Pulvis Gentianæ et Quassiæ.

℞   Gentianæ ....
       Quassiæ ....
       Cinnamomi ....āā...   ʒ ij
M.—Sig. Put in a pint of boiling water, and when cold, strain; dose, a wineglassful three times a day.

8.—Pulvis Juniperi Compositus.

℞   Juniperi ....
       Potassii bitartratis...............āā...   ʒ j
M. et ft. chart. No. 1.—Sig. Put in a pint of boiling water, and when cold, strain; dose, a wineglassful three times a day, before meals.

9.—Pulvis Anthemidis et Quassiæ.

℞ Anthemidis ....
Quassiæ...........................āā...   ʒ j

M. et ft. chart. No. 1.—Sig. Put in a pint of boiling water, and when cold, strain; dose, a wineglassful three times a day, before meals.

10.—Pulvis Calumbæ Compositus.

℞ Calumbæ ....
Zingiberis..........................āā...   ʒ ss
Sennæ ....   ʒ ij

M. et ft. chart. No. 1.—Sig. Put in a pint of boiling water, and when cold, strain; dose, a wineglassful three times a day.

11.—Pulvis Cimicifugæ Compositus.

℞ Cimicifugæ ....   ʒ j
Gentianæ ....
Zingiberis........................āā...   ʒ j

M. et ft. chart. No. 1.—Sig. Put in a pint of boiling water, and when cold, strain; dose, a wineglassful three times a day.

12.—Pulvis Potassii Bromidi Compositus.

℞ Potassii bromidi........................   ʒ j
Ferri sulphatis exsiccatæ..............   ʒ ss
Calumbæ................................
Zingiberis........................āā...   ʒ iv

M. et ft. chart. No. 1.—Sig. Put in a pint of boiling water, and when cold, strain; dose, a tablespoonful three times a day.

13.—Pulvis Hydrargyri et Sodii.

℞ Hydrargyri chloridi mitis............. gr. ⅓
   Sodii bicarbonatis..................... gr. x
Ft. chart. No. 1.

14.—Pulvis Cinchoniæ et Pepsinæ.

℞ Cinchoniæ sulphatis..................
   Pepsinæ.............................āā... gr. iij
M. et ft. chart. No. 1.

15.—Pulvis Ammonii Chloridi.

℞ Ammonii chloridi....................
   Ext. glycyrrhizæ...................āā... ℥ ij
M. et ft. chart. No. 1.—Sig. Put in ½ pint of water;
dose, a tablespoonful four times a day.

16.—Pulvis Cinchonidiæ Compositus.

℞ Cinchonidiæ sulphatis................ gr. ij
   Extr. glycyrrhizæ.................... gr. iij
   Sacchari............................. gr. v
M. et ft. chart. No. 1.

---o---

SUPPOSITORIA.

1.—Suppositorium Morphiæ.

℞ Morphiæ sulphatis.................... gr. ss
   Ol. theobromæ..............,......... q. s.
Ft. suppos. No. 1.

2.—Suppositorium Iodoformi.

℞ Iodoformi...................................... gr. v
   Ol. theobromæ............................ q. s.
   Ft. suppos. No. 1.

3.—Suppositorium Morphiæ et Belladonnæ.

℞ Morphiæ sulphatis........................ gr. ss
   Ext. belladonnæ.......................... gr. j ss
   Ol. theobromæ............................ q s.
   Ft. suppos. No. 1.

4.—Suppositorium Morphiæ Astringens.

℞ Morphiæ sulphatis........................ gr. ss
   Ext. belladonnæ.......................... gr. j ss
   Acidi tannici............................. gr. v
   Ol. theobromæ...... .... q. s.
   Ft. suppos. No. 1.

5.—Suppositorium Morphiæ Compositum.

℞ Sodii boratis............................. gr. v
   Morphiæ sulphatis........................ gr. ss
   Ext. belladonnæ.......................... gr. j ss
   Ol. theobromæ...... .... q. s.
   Ft. suppos. No. 1.

6.—Suppositorium Aeidi Tannici.

℞ Acidi tannici............................. gr. v
   Ol. theobromæ............................ q. s.
   Ft. suppos. No. 1.

TINCTURÆ.

1.—Tinctura Iodinii et Opii.

℞ Tr. iodinii............................... f ʒ vj
   Tr. opii................................ f ʒ ij
   M.—S. For external use.

2.—Tinctura Saponis Viridis.

℞ Saponis viridis......................... ʒ j
   Alcoholis............................... f ʒ ss
   M.—Dissolve and filter. For external use, with water.

—o—

UNGUENTA.

1.—Unguentum Diachyli.

℞ Plumbi oxidi........................... ʒ j ss
   Ol. olivæ.............................. ʒ vj ss
   The oil should be first mixed with water and heated;
then, while fresh water is poured in and the mixture
stirred, the oxide of lead is gradually added.

2.—Unguentum Belladonnæ Compositum.

℞ Ext. belladonnæ........................ gr. x
   Ext. stramonii......................... ʒ ss
   Acidi tannici.......................... gr. viij
   Adipis .... ʒ j
   M.

3.—Unguentum Hydrargyri Compositum.

℞   Ungt. hydrargyri.......................
      Ungt. belladonnæ......................
      Ungt. iodinii....................āā...   ʒ ij
M.

4.—Unguentum Veratriæ.

℞   Veratriæ.............. .... ℈ ij
      Adipis.................................. ʒ j
M. et ft. ungt.

5.—Unguentum Hydrargyri Oxidi Flavi.

℞   Hydrargyri oxidi flavi................. gr. xvj
      Ungt. petrolei....................... ʒ j
M.

6.—Unguentum Hydrargyri Ammoniati.

℞   Hyrargyri ammoniati................. gr. lxxx
      Ungt. petrolei....................... ʒ j
M.

PRESCRIBING MANUAL

OF THE

DISPENSARY

OF THE

Hospital of the Protestant Episcopal Church

OF

PHILADELPHIA.

——

☞ In prescribing, the Physician will write the *number* of the prescription, its *title*, the quantity to be dispensed, and the *directions* for using, *e. g* :—

For...

℞   No 2.—Liquor Potassii Bromidi, f ℥ iij
Sig One teaspoonful, diluted, three times a day.
Date.   *Signature.*

☞ Unless otherwise directed, the apothecary will always dispense three fluid ounces (f ℥ iij) of the fluid preparations, when the dose ordered is one fluid drachm (f ℨ j), and six fluid ounces (f ℥ vj) when the dose is half a fluid ounce (f ℥ ss).

·MEDICINES
FOR
INTERNAL ADMINISTRATION.

NOTE.—The following formulæ are designed for *adults* only.

LIQUORES.

1.—Liquor Potassii Bromidi (Nervous Sedative.)

℞ Potassii bromidi....................... gr. v
Aquæ.. f℥ j
M.—Dose, f℥ j–iv, diluted, three times daily.

MISTURÆ.

2.—Mistura Arsenicalis (Alterative).

℞ Liq. potassii arsenitis.................. ℳ v
Infus. gentianæ comp...... q. s...ad. f℥ j
M.—Dose, f℥ j, diluted, thrice daily, after meals.

3.—Mistura Hydrargyri et Ferri Chloridi.

℞ Hydrargyri chloridi corrosivi........ gr. 1-24
T nct. ferri chloridi..................... ℳ v
Infus. gentianæ comp.......q. s...ad. f℥ j
M.—Dose, f℥ j, diluted, thrice daily.

4—Mistura Potassii Iodidi (*a*).

℞ Potassii iodidi........................... gr. v
Infus. gentianæ comp................... f℥ j
M.—Dose, f℥ j–iv, diluted, thrice daily.

5.—Mistura Potassii Iodidi (*b*).

℞ Potassii iodidi.............................   gr v
    Vini colchici seminis..................   ℥ x
    Tinct. guaiaci ammoniat..............   ℥ xx
    Tinct. gentianæ comp......q. s...ad.   f ℨ j
M.—Dose, f ℨ j–ij, three or four times daily.

6.—Mistura Creasoti (Antacid).

℞ Aquæ creasoti............................   f ℨ j
    Sodii bicarbonatis.......................   gr. x
    Misturæ cretæ.................q. s...ad.   f ℥ ss
M.—Dose, f ℥ ss, three times a day.

7.—Mistura Sodii Bicarbonatis (*a*).

℞ Sodii bicarbonatis.......................   gr. x
    Tinct. gentianæ comp...................   f ℨ j
    Aquæ..........................q. s...ad.   f ℥ ss
M.—Dose, f ℥ ss, three times a day.

8.—Mistura Sodii Bicarbonatis (*b*).

℞ . Sodii bicarbonatis.......................   gr. v
    Sp. ammon. aromat....................   ℥ xx
    Aq. menthæ pip............q s...ad.   f ℨ j
M.—Dose, f ℨ j–ij, three times a day.

9.—Mistura Acidi Salicylici (Antipyretic).

℞ Acidi salicylici............................
    Sodii bicarbonatis.............āā...   gr. v
    Aquæ......................................   ℥ xl
M. et adde—
    Tinct. aurantii cort.....................   ℥ v
    Glycerinæ.................................   ℥ xv
M.—Dose, f ℨ j, every two or three hours.

10.—Mistura Lobeliæ Comp. (Antispasmodic)

℞ Tinct. lobeliæ............................ ♏ x
Tr. hyoscyami............................ ♏ xxx
Sp ætheris comp........................ ♏ x
Syr. tolutani....................q. s...ad. f ʒ j
M.—Dose, f ʒ j, every three hours.

11.—Mistura Acidi Sulphurici (*a*—Astringent)

℞ Acidi sulphurici aromat............... ♏ x
Tinct. opii deodoratæ .... ♏ v
Syrupi rubi.............................. f ʒ j
Aquæ...........................q. s...ad. f ʒ ij
M.—Dose, f ʒ ij, every three or four hours.

12.—Mistura Cretæ Comp.

℞ Tr. opii.................................... ♏ v
Tinct. krameriæ........................ f ʒ j
Spt. lavandulæ comp.................. ♏ xv
Mist. cretæ.................q. s...ad. f ℥ ss
M.—Dose, f ℥ ss, every three or four hours.

13.—Mistura Pepsinæ Comp. (Digestant.)

℞ Pepsinæ.................................... gr. x
Ac. muriatici dil........................ ♏ xv
Syrupi .... f ʒ ss
Aquæ........ ....q. s...ad. f ʒ ij
M.—Dose, f ʒ ij, diluted, thrice daily.

14.—Mistura Digitalis Comp. (Diuretic).

℞ Tinct. digitalis............................ ♏ v
Potassii acetatis........................ gr. xx
Spt. ætheris nitrosi..................... f ʒ j
Aquæ...........................q. s...ad. f ʒ ss
M.—Dose, f ʒ ss, three times a day.

15.—Mistura Ammon. Comp. (Expectorant).

℞ Copaibæ................................ ♏ v
Ext. glycyrrhizæ pulv.................. gr. x
Ol. anisi................................ ♏ ij
Misturæ ammoniaci.........q. s...ad. f ʒ j
M.—Dose, f ʒ j, every three or four hours.

16.—Mistura Ammonii Chloridi (*a*).

℞ Ammonii chloridi..................... gr. v
Mist. glycyrrhizæ comp.............. f ʒ j
M.—Dose, f ʒ j-ij, every two or three hours.

17.—Mistura Ammonii Chloridi (*b*).

℞ Ammon. chloridi...................... gr. v
Potassii iodidi......................... gr. ij
Glycerinæ.............................. ♏ xx
Syr. senegæ........................... ♏ xv
Aquæ...........................q. s...ad. f ʒ j
M.—Dose, f ʒ j, every two or three hours.

18.—Mistura Potassii Cyanidi.

℞ Potassii cyanidi........................
Morphiæ sulph..................āā... gr. 1-16
Syr. tolutani........................... f ʒ ss
Aquæ...........................q. s...ad. f ʒ j
Dose, f ʒ j, every six hours.

19.—Mistura Ergotæ Comp.(*a*—Hæmostatic).

℞   Ex. ergotæ fluidi............................ ℞ xx
     Tinct. digitalis............................ ℞ ij ss
     Tinct. opii deodorat...................... ℞ iij
     Aquæ cinnamomi............q. s...ad. f ℥ j

M.—Dose, f ℥ j, every one, two or three hours.

20.—Mistura Ergotæ Comp. (*b*).

℞   Ex. ergotæ fluidi........................ f ℥ ss
     Potassii bromidi.......................... gr. xv
     Aquæ cinnamomi............q. s...ad. f ℥ j

M.—Dose, f ℥ j–ij, p. r. n.

21.—Mistura Ferri Acida (Laxative and Cathartic).

℞   Ferri sulphatis........................... gr. j
     Magnesii sulphatis....................... gr. xl
     Acidi sulphurici dil...................... ℞ vij
     Infus. quassiæ................q. s...ad. f ℥ ss

M. —Dose, f ℥ ss, once or twice daily, well diluted.

22.—Mistura Sodii Bicarbonatis (*c*).

℞   Sodii bicarbonatis.......................
     Aloes socotrinæ...................āā... gr. x
     Spirit. lavandulæ comp................ f ℥ ss
     Aquæ............................q. s...ad. f ℥ ss

M.—Dose, f ℥ ij-iv, once or twice daily.

23.—Mistura Ammonii Carbonatis (*a*—Stimulant.)

℞   Ammon. carbonatis...................... gr. v
     Syr. tolutani............................. f ℥ ss
     Mucilag. acaciæ..............q. s...ad. f ℥ j

M.—Dose, f ℥ j-ij, every three hours.

24.—Mistura Nitro-Muriatici (Tonic and Antiperiodic).

℞   Acidi nitro·muriatici dil...............   ℳ x
     Infus. gentianæ comp......q, s...ad.   f ℥ j

M.—Dose, f ℥ j, diluted, three times daily.

25.—Mistura Cinchonidiæ.

℞   Cinchonidiæ sulphatis................   gr. ij
     Acidi sulphurici dil....................   ℳ iv
     Aquæ.........................q. s...ad.   f ℥ j

M.—Dose, f ℥ j–ij.

26.—Mistura Ferri Acetatis.

℞   Liquor ammonii acetatis..............   f ℥ j, ℳ xl
     Acidi acetici dil......................
     Tinct. ferri chloridi............āā...   ℳ x

M.—Dose, f ℥ j–ij, three or four times a day.

27.—Mist. Ferri Acetat. et Strychniæ.

℞   Strychniæ sulphatis....................   gr. 1-30
     Mist. ferri acetatis....................   f ℥ ij

M.—Dose, f ℥ j–ij, thrice daily.

28.—Mistura Ferri Comp.

℞   Strychniæ sulphatis......... ....   gr. 1-60
     Cinchoniæ sulphatis....................   gr. ij
     Tinct. ferri chloridi..................   ℳ x
     Acidi muriatici dil....................   ℳ v
     Aquæ.........................q. s...ad.   f ℥ j

M.—Dose, f ℥ j, diluted, thrice daily.

29.—Mistura Gentianæ Comp.

℞ Ferri et ammonii citratis............... gr. x
   Tinct. gentianæ comp.................. f ℥ j
   Spirit. lavandulæ comp............... f ℥ j
   Syrupi...................................... f ℥ j
   Aquæ...........................q. s...ad. f ℥ ss
   M.—Dose, f ℥ ss, three times daily.

30.—Mistura Strychniæ (*a*).

℞ Strychniæ sulph......................... gr. 1-48
   Acidi muriatici dil..................... ♏ x
   Syrupi simplicis......................... ♏ xx
   Aquæ............................q. s...ad. f ℥ ij
   M.—Dose, f ℥ ij, diluted, thrice daily.

31.—Mistura Strychniæ (*b*).

℞ Strychniæ sulphatis.................... gr. 1-48
   Ac. phosphorici dil.................... ♏ xx
   Syrupi simplicis........................ ♏ xx
   Aquæ...........................q. s...ad. f ℥ j
   Dose, f ℥ j, diluted, thrice daily.

PILULÆ.

32.—Pilula Zinci Oxidi (Anticolliquative).

℞ Zinci oxidi.............................. gr. iij
   Ex. belladonnæ........................ gr. ss
   M. et ft. pil. no. j.—Dose, one pill at night.

33.—Pilula Quiniæ et Digitalis (Antipyretic).

℞   Quiniæ sulphatis........................   gr. ij
     Pulv. digitalis............................   gr. ss
     Pulv. opii.................................   gr. ¼

   M. et ft. pil. no. j.—Dose, one pill every six hours.

34.—Pilula Argenti Nitratis (Astringent).

℞   Argenti nitratis........................   gr. 1-6
     Ext. gentianæ..........................   gr j

   M. et ft. pil. no. j.—Dose, one pill every four or six hours.

35.—Pilula Argenti Nitrat. et Opii.

℞   Argenti nitratis........................
     Pulv. opii......................āā...   gr. ¼
     Ext. gentianæ..........................   gr. j

   M. et ft. pil. no. j.—Dose, one pill every four or six hours.

36.—Pilula Cupri Sulphatis.

℞   Cupri sulphatis........................   gr. 1-6
     Pulv. opii.................................   gr. 1-6
     Ext. gentianæ..........................   gr. j

   M. et ft. pil. no. j.—Dose, one pill every four or six hours.

37.—Pilula Colocynth Comp. (Cathartic).

R   Ex. colocynth comp...................... gr. ij
    Res. podophyllin........................ gr. ⅛
    Ex. belladonnæ......................... gr. 1-6
    Ex. gentianæ........................... gr. j
    Olei carui.............................. gtt. ss

M. et ft. pil. no. j.—Dose, one pill at night, or night and morning.

——o——

PULVERES.

38.—Pulvis Sodii Comp. (Antacid).

R   Sodii bicarbonatis...................... gr. v
    Bismuthi subcarbonatis................ gr x

M. et ft. chart. no. j.—Dose, one powder thrice daily.

39.—Pulvis Kameelæ (Anthelmintic).

R   Pulv. kameelæ......................... ℨ j
Ft. chart. no. j.—Dose, one or two at night, or night and morning.

40.—Pulvis Bismuthi (Astringent).

R   Bismuthi subnitratis................... Ə j
Ft. chart. no. j.—Dose, one powder thrice daily.

41.—Pulvis Bismuthi et Ipecac.

R   Bismuthi subnitratis................... gr. x
    Pulv. ipecac. comp.................... gr. iij

M. et ft. chart. no. j.—Dose, one powder every three or four hours.

42.—Pulvis Bismuthi et Morphiæ.

℞   Bismuthi subnitratis........................   gr. x
     Morphiæ sulphatis........................   gr. ⅛
   M. et ft. chart. no. j.—Dose, one every four or six
hours.

43.—Pulvis Bismuthi et Pepsinæ (Digestant)

℞   Bismuthi subnitratis....................
     Pepsinæ ....āā...   gr. x
   M. et ft. chart. no. j.—Dose, one powder thrice daily.

44.—Pulvis Sodii et Pepsinæ.

℞   Sodii bicarbonatis........................   gr. v
     Pepsinæ..................................   gr. x
   M. et ft. chart. no. j.—Dose, one powder thrice daily.

45.—Pulvis Buchu Comp. (Diuretic).

℞   Foliæ buchu...........................
     Foliæ uvæ ursi........................
     Sem, lini.....................āā...   ℥ j
     Sodii bicarbonatis.............. ....   ℥ ss
   M. et ft. chart. no. j.—Sig. Add two pints of boiling
water; when cold, strain.   Dose, a wineglassful thrice
daily.

MEDICINES

FOR

CHILDREN.

In the following formulæ the doses have been propor·
tioned for children who have reached the age of two
years:

MISTURÆ.

46.—Mistura Olei Morrhuæ (Alterative).

℞ Olei morrhuæ............................ f℥ ss
   Syr. calcii lacto-phosphat..............
   Aquæ calcis........................āā... ℳ xv
   M.—Dose, f℥ j–ij, three times daily

47.—Mistura Potassii Arsenitis.

℞ Liquor potassii arsenitis.............. ℳ ij
   Syr. simplicis........................... f℥ ss
   Aquæ...........................q. s...ad. f℥ j
   M.—Dose, f℥ j, thrice daily.

48.—Mistura Potassii Iodidi (c).

℞ Potassii iodidi......................... gr. j
   Syr. sarsap. comp.....................
   Aquæ ....āā... f℥ ss
   M.—Dose, f℥ j–ij, thrice daily.

49.—Mistura Antacida (Antacid).

℞   Liquor calcis...........................
      Aq. cinnamomi....................āā...   f ʒ ss

M.—Dose, f ʒ j–ij, every one, two or three hours.

50.— Mistura Sodii et Rhei.

℞   Sodii bicarbonatis........................   gr. ij
      Syr. rhei aromat.........................   ♏ xv
      Aq. menth. pip...............q. s...ad.   f ʒ j

M.—Dose, f ʒ j, every two or three hours.

51.-Mistura Chloral. Hydrat.(Antispasmodic)

℞   Chloral. hydrat...........................   gr. ij
      Potass. bromidi..........................   gr. v
      Syr. simplicis...........................
      Aquæ..........................āā...   f ʒ ss

M.—Dose, f ʒ j, p. r. n.

52.—Mistura Belladonnæ.

℞   Tinct. belladonnæ.......................   ♏ ij
      Potassii bromidi........................   gr. v
      Syrupi simplicis.........................   f ʒ ss
      Aquæ.......................q. s...ad.   f ʒ j

M.—Dose, f ʒ j, p. r. n.

53.—Mistura Acidi Sulphurici (*b*—Astringent)

℞   Acidi sulphurici dil......................   ♏ ij
      Liquor morphiæ sulph..................   ♏ viij
      Elix. Curaçoæ...........................   ♏ v
      Aquæ.......................q. s...ad.   f ʒ j

M.— Dose, f ʒ j, every three or four hours.

54.—Mistura Bismuthi.

℞ Bismuthi subnitratis......................... gr. vj
   Tr. opii deodorat......................... ♏ j
   Syrupi simplicis......................... ♏ xx
   Mist. cretæ.....................q. s...ad. f ʒ j

M.—Dose, f ʒ j, every two or three hours.

55.—Mistura Antifebrilis (Diaphoretic).

℞ Potassii citratis......................... gr. ij
   Spt. ætheris nitrosi.....................
   Syr. limonis.....................āā... ♏ x
   Liquor ammon. acetat......q. s...ad. f ʒ j

M.—Dose, f ʒ j, every two or three hours.

56.—Mistura Pepsinæ (Digestant).

℞ Pepsinæ saccharat......................... gr. iij
   Acidi muriatici dil..................... ♏ iij
   Glycerinæ .... ♏ v
   Aquæ.....................q. s...ad. f ʒ j

M.—Dose, f ʒ j, three times daily.

57.—Mistura Potassii Acetatis (Diuretic.)

℞ Potassii acetatis......................... gr. ij ss
   Sp. juniperis comp..................... ♏ v
   Sp. ætheris nitrosi..................... ♏ x
   Syr. simplicis............,............. ♏ xx
   Aquæ.....................q. s...ad. f ʒ j

M.—Dose, f ʒ j, every three or four hours.

58.—Mistura Ammon. Carbonat. (*b*).

℞ Ammon. carbonatis...................... gr. j
    Syrup tolutan... ....
    Syr   acaciæ............................
    Aquæ...........................āā... ℳ xx
M.—Dose, one teaspoonful every two or three hours.

59.—Mist. Ammonii Chloridi (*c*-Expectorant)

℞ Syr. ipecacuanhæ....................... ℳ v
    Ammonii chloridi....................... gr. ij
    Syr. tolutan............................ f ℨ ss
    Aquæ...........................q. s... f ℨ j
M.—Dose, f ℨ j, every three hours.

60.—Mistura Ipecac. Comp.

℞ Vini ipecacuanhæ....................... ℳ iij
    Sp. ætheris nitrosi.....................
    Tr. opii camphorat..............āā... ℳ iv
    Syrupi tolutani......................... ℳ x
    .Liq. ammonii acetatis......q. s...ad. f ℨ j
M.—Dose, f ℨ j, every three hours.

61.—Mistura Aloes et Ferri (Laxative and Cathartic).

℞ Tinct. aloes et ferri..................... ℳ x
    Ferri sulphatis exsiccat................ gr. 1-6
    Syr. rhei aromat.............q. s...ad. f ℨ j
M.—Dose, f ℨ j, thrice daily.

62.—Mistura Magnesii et Opii.

R Magnesii sulphatis...................... gr. v
Tr. opii deodorat........................ m ss
Syrupi................................. m x
Aq. menth. pip...............q. s...ad. f℥ j
M.—Dose, f℥ j, every three hours.

63.—Mistura Ferri et Cinchonidiæ (Tonic and Antiperiodic).

R Cinchonidiæ sulphatis................. gr. j
Tinct. ferri chloridi.................... m ij
Syr. zingiberis.......................... f℥ ss
Aquæ.....................q. s...ad. f℥ j
M.—Dose, f℥ j, thrice daily, diluted.

64.—Mistura Potassii Chlorat. (a).

R Potassii chloratis...................... gr. ij ss
Tinct. ferri chloridi.................... m ij ss
Ac. muriatici dil....................... m ij
Syr. zingiberis.......................... f℥ ss
Aquæ.....................q. s...ad. f℥ j
M.—Dose, f℥ j, every two or three hours.

65.—Mistura Potassii Chlorat. (b).

R Potassii chloratis...................... gr. ij
Acidi muriatici dil..................... m ij
Glycerinæ .... m x
Aquæ.....................q.s...ad. f℥ j
M.—Dose, f℥ j, three to five times daily, in water.

PULVERES.

66.—Pulvis Hydrarg. et Sodii (Antacid).

℞   Hydrarg. chloridi mit...................   gr. 1-10
     Sodii bicarbonatis.......................   gr. ij
     M. et ft. chart. no. j.—Dose, one every 2 or 3 hours.

67.—Pulvis Sodii et Bismuthi.

℞   Sodii bicarbonatis......................   gr. iij
     Bismuthi subcarbonatis...............   gr. ij
     M. et ft. chart. no. j.—Dose, one powder thrice daily.

68.—Pulvis Santonini (Anthelmintic).

℞   Santonini..................................   gr. ss
     Sacch. albi...............................   gr. j ss
     M. et ft. chart. no. j.—Dose, one or two powders
morning and evening, the second to be followed by a purge.

69.—Pulvis Bismuthi et Opii (Astringent).

℞   Bismuthi subnitratis....................   gr. v
     Pulv. opii.................................   gr. 1-12
     M. et ft. chart no. j.—Dose, one powder every 3 hours.

70.—Pulvis Cretæ Præparatæ Comp.

℞   Cretæ præparatæ.......................   gr. iv
     Pulv. ipecac co........................   gr. ss
     Pulv. aromat............................   gr. ss
     M. et ft. chart. no. j.—Dose, one powder every two or
three hours.

71.—Pulvis Hydrarg. Chloridi Mit. (Laxative)

℞   Hydrarg. chloridi mitis................   gr. j
     Sacchari albi............................   gr. ⁙
     M. et ft. chart. no. j.—Dose, one powder.

PREPARATIONS

FOR

EXTERNAL USE.

The various fluid preparations embraced in this list are to be kept and dispensed in *colored* and *roughened* bottles, labelled "*For External Use.*"

GARGARISMATA.

72.—Gargarisma Potass. Chlorat. et Acidi Carbolici.

℞   Potassii chloratis.......................   gr. xx
     Acidi carbolici..........................   gr. v
     Glycerinæ .... $\mathfrak{m}$ lxxx
     Aquæ.....................q. s...ad.   f ℥ j
    M.—Sig. Add, f ℥ ss to f ℥ iv of water.

73.—Gargarisma Potass. Chlorat. et Ferri.

℞   Potass. chloratis.......................   gr. xx
     Tinct. ferri chloridi....................
     Ac. muriatici dil.................āā... $\mathfrak{m}$ xx
     Aquæ.....................q. s...ad.   f ℥ j
    M.—Sig. Add f ℥ ss to f ℥ iv of water.

74.—Gargarisma Sodii Biboratis.

℞   Sodii biboratis..........................   gr. xv
     Glycerinæ...............................   f ℥ ij
     Aquæ..... ....q. s...ad.   f ℥ j
    M.

GLYCERITA.

75.—Glyceritum Tr. Ferri Chloridi.

℞ Tinct. ferri chloridi......................
Glycerinæ.........................āā... f ℥ ss
M.

76.—Glyceritum Iodinii.

℞ Liq. iodinii comp.......................
Glycerinæ.........................āā... f ℥ ss
M.

—o—

LINIMENTA.

77.—Linimentum Aconiti Comp.

℞ Tinct. aconiti rad.....................
Chloroformi...........................
Tr. opii..............................
Olei olivæ.......................āā... f ℥ j
Lin. saponis camph.........q. s...ad. f ℥ j
M.

78.—Linimentum Stimulans.

℞ Olei terebinthinæ...................... f ℥ ij
Lin. ammoniæ.......................... f ℥ iv
M.

—o—

LIQUORES.

79.—Liquor Acidi Carbolici (a).

℞ Acidi carbolici......................... gr. v
Aquæ.................................. f ℥ j
M.

80.—Liquor Acidi Carbolici (b).

℞ Acidi carbolici........................... gr. xx
   Aquæ..................................... f℥ j
M.

81.—Liquor Argenti Nitratis (a).

℞ Argenti nitratis......................... gr. ij
   Aquæ destillat........................... f℥ j
M.

82.—Liquor Argenti Nitratis (b).

℞ Argenti nitratis......................... gr. x
   Aquæ destillat........................... f℥ j
M.

83.—Liquor Argenti Nitratis (c).

℞ Argenti nitratis......................... gr. xxx
   Aquæ destillat........................... f℥ j
M.

84.—Liquor Atropiæ (a).

℞ Atropiæ sulphatis....................... gr. ss
   Aquæ destillat........................... f℥ j
M.

85.—Liquor Atropiæ (b).

℞ Atropiæ sulphatis....................... gr. iv
   Aquæ destillat........................... f℥ j
M.

86.—Liquor Zinci Sulphatis.

℞   Zinci sulphatis..............................   gr. ij
      Aquæ destillat............................   f ℥ j
   M.

87.—Liquor Zinci et Aluminis.

℞   Zinci sulphatis............................
      Pulv. aluminis.....................āā...   gr. ij
      Aquæ......................................   f ℥ j
   M.

88.—Liquor Plumbi Acetat. et Opii.

℞   Tr. opii.....................................   f ℥ j ,
      Liq. plumbi subacetat..................   f ℥ ss
      Aquæ..........................q. s...ad.   f ℥ j
   M.

—o—

PULVERES.

89.—Pulvis Aluminis et Zinci.

℞   Pulv. aluminis...........................   ℥ ss
      Zinci sulphatis...........................   ℥ j
   M.—Sig. Dissolve in one quart of water.

90.—Pulv. Plumbi. Acetat. et Zinci.

℞   Plumbi acetatis..........................   ℥ j
      Zinci acetatis............................   ℥ j
   M.—Sig. Dissolve in a quart of water.

91.—Pulvis Querc. Alb. et Zinci.

℞   Querci albæ...................... ....   ℥ j
     Zinci sulphatis...........................   ℥ j

M.—Sig. Add a quart of boiling water, let stand for two hours, and strain.

92.—Pulvis Quassiæ.

℞   Quassiæ ligni...........................   ℥ ij

Sig. Add one pint of boiling water, let stand till cold, and strain.

—o—

UNGUENTA.

93.—Unguentum Diachyli.

℞   Lithargyri...............................   ℥ ij
     Olei olivæ..............................   f℥ j

Coque, dein adde—

     Olei lavandulæ........... ....   ♏ iv

M. et ft. ung.

94.—Ung. Iodinii et Belladonnæ.

℞   Ung. iodin. comp.......................
     Ung. belladonnæ.......................
     Ung. hydrarg....................āā...   ℥ ss

M. et ft ung.

95.—Ung. Iodoformi.

℞   Iodoformi................................. $\frac{3}{3}$ j
      Adipis......................................   j
  M. et ft. ung.

96.—Ung. Stramonii et Ac. Tannici.

℞   Ung. stramonii...........................
      Ung. ac. tannici....................āā...   ℥ ss
  M. et ft. ung.

PHARMACOPŒIA

OF THE

PHILADELPHIA HOSPITAL.

CHARTÆ.

Charta Arsenicalis Composita.

℞ Belladonnæ foliæ........................ gr. xcvj
Hyoscyami foliæ........................
Stramonii foliæ....................āā... gr. xlviij
Extracti opii............................ gr. iv
Tabaci foliæ............................ gr. lxxx

Fiat infusum, et adde—

Potassii nitratis........................ gr. clx
Potassii arsenitis....................... gr. cccxx

Fiat solutio, et—

Saturate bibulous paper and dry for use.

GLYCERITA.

Glyceritæ Olei Ricini.

℞ Olei cinnamomi.......................... gtt. xxiv
Olei ricini.................................
Glycerini ....āā... f ℥ iv
Misce.

INFUSA.

Infusum Sennæ Compositum.

℞ Sennæ foliæ............................... ℥ viij
Pulveris jalapæ.......................... ℥ iij
Potassæ bitartratis..................... ℥ ij
Aquæ bullientis......................... O vj
Macera per horas duas, cola, et adde—
Tincturæ sennæ compositi............ O ij
Misce —Signa.   Dose, a tablespoonful.

LINIMENTA.

Linimentum Chloroformi Compositum.

℞ Chloroformi.............................. f ℥ ij
Tincturæ aconiti radicis...............
Aquæ ammoniæ...................āā... f ℥ ss
Olei olivæ................................. f ℥ v
Fiat linimenta.

Linimentum Saponis Viride.

℞ Saponis viridis............................ ℥ j
   Alcoholis................................... q. s.

Fiat solutio. Liquefac cum leni calore. Misce ci filtra.

Linimentum Terebinthinæ Compositum.

℞ Olei terebinthinæ..........................
   Aquæ ammoniæ fortioris........āā... f℥ j
   Linimentum saponis.................... f℥ iv

Fiat linimenta.

—o—

LIQUORES.

Liquor Bromini.

℞ Bromini .... ℥ j
   Aquæ .... f℥ ij
   Potassii bromidi......................... q. s.

Fiat solutio. Signa. For physicians' use, only.

Liquor Plumbi Subacetatis cum Opii (Lead-water and Laudanum).

℞ Tincturæ opii........................... f℥ ji
   Liquoris plumbi subacetatis, diluti
                 q. s...ad. O ij

Misce.

MISTURÆ.

Mistura Antirheumatica.

℞ Potassæ nitratis............................ ℥ j
Vini colchici radicis..................... f℥ j
Spiritus ætheris nitrosi.................. f℥ j
Syrupi guiaci............................. f℥ ij
Olei gaultheriæ.......................... gtt. vj
Aquæ....................q. s...ad. f℥ vj

Misce.—Signa. Dose, a tablespoonful every two hours.

Mistura Arsenicalis Composita.

℞ Liquoris arsenici chloridi............ .... f℥ ss
Tincturæ ferri chloridi................. f℥ j ss
Cinchoniæ sulphatis.................... ℥ ij
Strychniæ sulphatis.................... gr. ij
Syrupi.....................................
Aquæ.................āā...q. s...ad. f℥ vj

Fiat mistura. Signa—Dose, a teaspoonful.

Mistura Astringens.

℞ Acidi sulphurici aromatici............ f℥ ij
Extracti hæmatoxyli................... ℥ ij
Tincturæ opii camphoratæ............ f℥ ss
Syrupi zingiberis............q, s...ad. f℥ vj

Misce secundem artem.—Signa. Dose, a tablespoon-ful.

Mistura Cosmetica (Goddard's Cosmetic Lotion).

R̥ Tincturæ benzoini.................................... f℥ ij
Hydrargyri chloridi corrosivi......... gr. vj
Aquæ rosæ.................................... f℥ vj

Fiat mistura.

Mistura Cretæ Composita.

R̥ Tincturæ catechu.........................
Tincturæ opii camphoratæ......āā... f℥ vj
Acidi carbolici........................... gtt. xij
Mistura cretæ.................q. s...ad. f℥ vj

Misce secundem artem.—Signa.   Dose, a tablespoonful.

Mistura Ferri Chloridi Composita (Basham's Mixture).

R̥ Liqucris ammoniæ acetatis........... f℥ iij
Tincturæ ferri chloridi................. f℥ ij ss
Acidi acetici diluti..................... f℥ j
Curacæ, vel alcohol .... f℥ ij
Syrupi...............................,.........
Aquæ..................āā...q. s...ad.   f℥ vj

Fiat mistura.   Signa.—Dose, a tablespoonful.

Mistura Ferri cum Quiniæ.

R̥ Quiniæ sulphatis........................ ℥ j
Acidi phosphorici diluti.............. q. s.
Ferri pyrophosphatis................... ℥ ss
Mistura aromaticæ...........q. s...ad. f℥ xxx

Misce secundem artem.   Signa.—Dose, a tablespoonful—containing 1 gr. of quinia and 4 grs. of iron.

Mistura Sodæ (Soda Mint).

R Sodæ bicarbonatis........................   ʒ ij
Spiritus ammoniæ aromatici..........   gtt. xxxvj
Aquæ menthæ viridis..................   f ℥ viij

Misce.—Signa. Dose, one or two tablespoonfuls three times a day.

———

Mistura Sodæ Composita.

R Sodæ bicarbonatis......................   ʒ ij
Creasoti...................................   gtt. xij
Syrupi acaciæ...........................   f ℥ ij
Spiritus lavandulæ compositæ.......   f ℥ i ss
Aquæ.......................q. s...ad.   f ℥ vj

Fiat mistura. Signa.—Dose, tablespoonful two hours after meals.

———

Chlorodyne.

R Chloroformi.............................   f ℥ ss
Spiritus ætheris sulphurici............   f ℥ j ss
Olei menthæ piperiæ..................   gtt. viij
Oleoresinæ capsici....................   gtt. ij
Extracti cannabis Indicæ.............   gr. vj
Morphiæ muriatis.......................   gr. xvj
Acidi hydrocyanici diluti ....   ℳ lxv
Acidi hydrochlorici diluti.............   f ʒ j
Glycerinæ..................................
Mellis...................āā...q. s...ad.   f ℥ iv

Fiat mistura secundem artem. Signa.—Dose, 15 to 20 drops.

Mistura Zollickofferi (Zollickoffer's Mixture)

R   Potassii iodidi...........................
Pulveris guaiaciæ resin..........āā...   ℥ ij ss
Vini colchici radicis...................   f℥ j ss
Aquæ cinnamomi........................
Syrupi...................āā...q. s...ad.   O j

Fiat mistura. Signa.—Dose, a tablespoonful.

——o——

PILULÆ.

____

Pilulæ Aloes Compositæ.

R   Pulveris aloes socotrinæ...............   ℥ ss
Ferri sulphatis exsiccatæ.............
Terebinthinæ albæ...............āā...   ℥ ij

Misce, et fiant pilulæ cxx. Signa —Each pill contains
2 grs. of aloes, and 1 gr. each of iron and turpentine.

____

Pilulæ Antineuralgicæ.

R   Acidi arseniosi...........................   gr. iv
Strychniæ sulphatis.....................   gr. iij
Extracti belladonnæ...................   gr. xxiv
Cinchonæ sulphatis....................   ℥ iij
Pilulæ ferri carbonatis................   ℥ v

Misce, et fiant pilulæ cxx. Signa.—Each pill contains
1-30 gr. of arsenic, 1-40 gr. of strychnia, 1·5 gr. of belladonna, 1½ grs. of cinchonia, and 2½ grs. of iron.

Pilulæ Cinchoniæ et Arsenici.

R   Cinchoniæ sulphatis.....................
    Ferri redacti.......................āā...   ℥ ss
    Extracti nucis vomicæ.................   gr. xxx
    Acidi arseniosi...........................   gr. vj

Misce, et fiant pilulæ cxx. Signa.—Each pill contains
1-20 gr. of arsenic, ¼ gr. of nux vomica, and 2 grs.
each of iron and cinchonia.

Pilulæ Colocynthæ cum Belladonnæ.

R   Extracti belladonnæ....................   gr. xv
    Extracti colocynthidis compositæ...
    Pulveris aloes socotrinæ...........ūā...   ℥ iij .
    Olei anisi...................................   gtt. xxx

Misce, et fiant pilulæ cxx. Signa —Each pill contains
1-8 gr. of belladonna, and 1½ grs. each of aloes and
colocynth.

Pilulæ Opii cum Plumbi Acetatæ.

R   Pulveris opii..............................   gr. xl
    Plumbi acetatæ.........................   ℥ ss

Misce, et fiant pilulæ cxx. Signa.—Each pill contains
½ gr. of opium, and 2 grs. of acetate of lead.

Pilulæ Cinchoniæ Compositæ.

R   Cinchoniæ sulphatis....................
    Ferri redacti.......................āā...   ℥ ss
    Extracti nucis vomicæ.................   gr. xxx

Misce, et fiant pilulæ cxx. Signa.—Each pill contains
¼ gr. of nux vomica, and 2 grs. each of iron and cinchonia.

Pilulæ Podophylli Compositæ.

℞ Resinæ podophylli...................... gr. xx
Extracti colocynthidis composita....
Extracti hyoscyami...............āā... ℥ ij

Misce, et fiant pilulæ cxx. Signa.—Each pill contains
1·6 gr. of podophylliu, and 1 gr. each of colocynth and
hyoscyamus.

Pilulæ Rhei et Gentianæ.

℞ Pulveris rhei........................... ℥ ss
Extracti gentianæ.......................
Extracti hyoscyami.............āā... ℥ ij

Misce, et fiant pilulæ cxx. Signa.—Each pill contains
2 grs. of rhubarb, and 1 gr. each of gentian and hyoscyamus.

PULVERES.

Pulveris Glycyrrhizæ Composita.

℞ Pulveris sennæ...........................
Pulveris glycyrrhizæ radicis.....āā... ℥ vj
Pulveris fœniculi.......................
Sulphuris loti.....................āā... ℥ iij
Sacchari albæ........................... ℥ xviij

Misce.—Signa Dose, a teaspoonful at bed-time.

Pulveris Sodæ Composita.

℞ Bismuthi subnitratis.................... gr. v
Sodæ bicarbonatis.....................
Pulveris zingiberi....................
Pulveris calumbæ,,,,,,,,,,,,,,āā... gr. ij ss

Misce.

SYRUPI.

Syrupus Chlorali.

R   Chloral hydrat...................... ...... ℥ ij, ℨ v, ℈ j
       Tincturæ cardamomi................... f℥ j
       Syrupi..................................... f℥ iv
       Aquæ cinnamomi............q. s...ad.   O j

Misce.—Signa. A teaspoonful contains ten grains of chloral.

Syrupus Guaiaci.

R   Pulveris guaiaci resinæ............... ℈ xxxij
       Liquoris potassæ....................... f℥ ss
       Sacchari albæ........................... ℔ j (av.)
       Aquæ..................................... f℥ viij

Fiat syrupus. Signa.—Dose, a teaspoonful, containing five grs. of guaiacum.

Syrupus Pectoralis.

R   Ammoniæ muriatis..................... ℥ ss
       Syrupi senegæ......................... f℥ j
       Misturæ glycyrrhizæ comp..q. s..ad.   f℥ viij

Misce.—Signa. Dose, a dessertspoonful.

Syrupus Potassii Iodidi.

R   Potassii iodidi........................... ℥ j
       Syrupi sarsaparillæ comp...q. s...ad.   f℥ vj

Misce.—Signa. Dose, a dessertspoonful, containing twenty grains of potassa.

Syrupus Potassii Iodidi Composita.

℞ Hydrargyri chloridi corrosivi......... gr. ij
Potassii iodidi........................... ℥ j
Syrupi sarsaparillæ comp...q. s...ad. f ℥ vj

Misce.—Signa. Dose, a dessertspoonful, containing 1-12 gr. of mercury and twenty grs. of potassa.

—o—

TINCTURÆ.

Tinctura Aromatica.

℞ Coriandri fructus...................... ℥ ij
Angelicæ fructus...................... ℥ ij ss
Glycerinæ .... f ℥ v
Syrupi................................ f ℥ vj
Alcoholis diluti, q. s., ut fiant tinc-
tura................................. O ij

Signa.—A pleasant vehicle for administering nauseous remedies.

Tinctura Ferri Composita.

℞ Cinchoniæ sulphatis.................. ℥ j
Strychniæ sulphatis.................. gr. ij
Tincturæ ferri chloridi.............. f ℥ j
Syrupi....................................
Aquæ.................āā...q. s...ad. f ℥ viij

Misce secundem artem. Signa.—Dose, a teaspoonful three times a day.

Tinctura Saponis Viride cum Picis.

℞ Picis liquidæ...............................
Saponis viridis............................
Spiritus methlyci..................āā...   ℥ j
Misce cum leni calore.

———

Tinctura Styptica.

℞ Potassæ carbonatis......................   ℥ j
Saponis ....   ℥ ij
Alcoholis....................................   f℥ iv
Fiat mistura secundem artem.

——o——

UNGUENTA.

Unguentum Plumbi Oxidi.

℞ Emplastræ plumbi......................   ℥ j
Olei olivæ................................   f℥ ij
Misce cum leni calore.

———

Unguentum Zinci Oxidi Benzoatum.

℞ Zinci oxidi................................   ℥ j
Tincturæ benzoini......................   gtt. xl
Adipis ....   ℥ vij
Fiat unguentum.

PRESCRIBING MANUAL

OF THE

CHILDREN'S HOSPITAL

OF

PHILADELPHIA.

The *doses* of all the formulæ are proportioned for children who have reached the age of *two years*, one tea-spoonful (f℥j) being the dose of each preparation.

The following table represents the *doses* for different ages, apportioned according to this standard:

6 months and over, ¼ of a teaspoonful = f℥ ¼

1 year   "   ½   "   = f℥ ss

2 years   "   1 teaspoonful   = f℥ j

4   "   "   2 teaspoonfuls   = f℥ ij

8   "   "   4   "   = f℥ ss

In prescribing, the Physician will write the *number* of the Prescription, its *title*, the *record number* or *name* of the *patient*, and the *directions*, for using it, *e. g.*:—

℞

No. 1.

Liquor Cinchonidiæ Sulphatis.

S.

For No. 1000.

Teaspoonful four times daily.

Date.   *Signature.*

Unless otherwise directed, the apothecary will always dispense three fluid ounces (f ℥ iij) of the fluid preparations.

For convenience and certainty of measurement, when the *dose* to be prescribed is less than *one fluid drachm* (say f ʒ ¼ or f ʒ ss), the apothecary will dilute a proportional quantity (say f ʒ vj or f ℥ jss) of the mixture with sufficient of some suitable menstruum to raise the amount to *three fluid ounces* (f ℥ iij), and the patient will take of this *one teaspoonful* (f ʒ j).

MEDICINES

FOR

INTERNAL ADMINISTRATION.

LIQUORES.

Antiperiodic—

1.—Liquor Cinchonidiæ Sulphatis.

℞   Cinchonidiæ sulphatis................   gr. j
    Acidi sulphurici diluti......... ......   ℳ j
    Aquæ......................q. s...ad.   f ℥ j

M.—Dose, f ʒ j, three times a day.

2.—Liquor Quiniæ Sulphatis.

℞   Quiniæ sulphatis.........................   gr. j
     Acidi sulphurici diluti..................   ♏ j
     Aquæ......................q. s...ad.   f ʒ j
    M.—Dose, f ʒ j, three times a day.

Nervous Sedative—

3.—Liquor Potassii Bromidi.

℞   Potassii bromidi..........................   gr. ij ss
     Aquæ....................................   f ʒ j
    M.—Dose, f ʒ j, diluted, three times a day.

—o—

MISTURÆ.

Alterative—

4.—Mistura Arsenicalis.

℞   Liquor potassii arsenitis...............   ♏ ij
     Infus. gentianæ comp..................   f ʒ ss
     Aquæ......................q. s...ad.   f ʒ j
    M.—Dose, f ʒ j, three times daily.

5.—Mistura Ferro-Arsenicalis.

℞   Liquor arsenici chloridi...............
     Tr. ferri chloridi................āā...   ♏ ij
     Aquæ......................q. s...ad.   f ʒ j
    M.—Dose, f ʒ j, three times daily.

6.—Mistura Ferri Iodidi.

℞ Syr. ferri iodidi.......................   ♏ v
   Syrupi.....................q. s...ad.   f ℥ j
   M.—Dose, f ℥ j, three times daily.

7.—Mistura Hydrargyri Chloridi Corrosivi

℞ Hydrargyri chloridi corrosivi.........   gr. 1-96
   Syrupi....................................
   Aquæ........................āā...   f ℥ ss
   M.—Dose, f ℥ j, three times daily.

8.—Mistura Olei Morrhuæ.

℞ Olei morrhuæ...........................   f ℥ ss
   Syr. calcii lactophosphatis............   ♏ xv
   Liq. calcis....................q. s...ad.   f ℥ j
   M.—Dose, f ℥ j, three times daily.

9.—Mistura Olei Morrhuæ Comp.

℞ Olei morrhuæ...........................   f ℥ ss
   Syr. calcii lactophosphatis............   ♏ xv
   Syr. ferri iodidi.......................   ♏ iv
   Liquor calcis.................q. s...ad.   f ℥ j
   M.—Dose, f ℥ j, three times a day.

10.—Mistura Potassii Iodidi.

℞ Potassii iodidi...........................   gr. j.
   Syr. sarsap. comp......................
   Aquæ..............................āā...   f ℥ ss
   M.—Dose, f ℥ j, three times daily.

Antacid—
11.—Mistura Antacida.

℞ Liquor calcis.............................
Aquæ cinnamomi................āā... f℥ ss
M.—Dose, f℥j, every hour.

12.—Mistura Magnesii Carbonatis.

℞ Magnesii carbonatis.................... gr. j
Misturæ antacidæ (No. 11)........... f℥ j
M.—Dose, f℥j, every hour.

13.—Mistura Sodii Bicarbonatis.

℞ Sodii bicarbonatis..................... gr. ij
Syrupi.................................... ♏ xv
Aq. menth. pip...............q. s...ad. f℥ j
M.—Dose, f℥j, every three hours.

14.—Mistura Sodii et Gentianæ.

℞ Sodii bicarbonatis..................... gr. iij
Infus. gentianæ comp..................
Aquæ..............................āā... f℥ ss
M.—Dose, f℥j, three times daily.

15.—Mistura Sodii et Rhei.

℞ Sodii bicarbonatis..................... gr. ij
Syr. rhei aromat...................... ♏ x
Aq. menth. pip...............q s...ad. f℥ j
M.—Dose, f℥j, every three hours.

Anthelmintic—

16.—Mistura Kameelæ Comp.

Ŗ Kameelæ.................................... gr. **v**
   Syr. acaciæ.............................. f3 ss

Misce, et adde—

   Oleoresinæ filicis maris............... ℞ xv
   Aquæ.......................q. s...ad. f3 j

M.—Dose, f3 j, three times a day for one day.

———

17.—Mistura Olei Chenopodii.

Ŗ Ol. chenopodii.......................... ℞ iv
   Pulv. acaciæ............................ gr. x
   Syrupi................................... f3 ss
   Aquæ cinnamomi............q. s...ad. f3 j

M.—Dose, f3 j, three times a day for one day, to be
followed by a laxative.

———

18.—Mistura Olei Chenopodii Comp.

Ŗ Olei chenopodii........................ ℞ iv
   Olei ricini.............................. f3 ss
   Olei cinnamomi......................... ℞ ¼
   Syr. acaciæ..................q. s...ad. f3 j

M.—Dose, f3 j, three times a day.

———

19.—Mistura Oleoresinæ Filicis.

Ŗ Oleoresinæ filicis.......................
   Olei ricini.......................āā... ℞ xv
   Olei cinnamomi........................ ℞ ¼
   Syr. acaciæ..................q. s...ad. f3 j

M.—Dose, f3 j, three times a day for one day, to be
followed by a laxative if necessary.

Antiperiodic—

20.—Mistura Quiniæ Sulphatis.

℞   Quiniæ sulphatis........................   gr. j
     Acidi sulphurici dil ....   ♏ j
     Syr. zingiberis...........................   f ℥ ss
     Aquæ.........................q. s...ad.   f ℥ j

    M.—Dose, f ℥ j, three times a day.

Antispasmodic—

21.—Mistura Belladonnæ et Aluminis.

℞   Ext. belladonnæ........................   gr. 1-24
     Pulv. aluminis..........................   gr. ij
     Syr. zingiberis...........................
     Syr. acaciæ.............................
     Aquæ..............................āā...   ♏ xx

    M.—Dose, f ℥ j, every three hours.

Antipyretic—

22.—Mistura Acidi Salicylici.

℞   Acidi sallicylici..........................
     Sodii bicarbonatis................āā...   gr. j
     Aquæ......................................   ♏ xlviij

    M. et adde—

     Tr. aurantii cort........................   ♏ ij
     Glycerinæ ....   ♏ x

    M.—Dose, f ℥ j, p. r. n.

Astringent—

23.—Mistura Acidi Sulphurici.

℞   Acidi sulphurici dil...................   ℳ ij
     Liquor morphiæ sulph...............   ℳ viij
     Elix. Curaҫoæ...........................   ℳ v
     Aquæ.......................q. s...ad.   f ℨ j
   M.—Dose, f ℨ j, every three or four hours.

24.—Mistura Argenti Nitratis.

℞   Argenti nitratis..........................   gr. 1-64
     Syr. acaciæ.............................   ℳ x
     Aquæ.......................q. s...ad.   f ℨ j
   M.—Dose, f ℨ j, every three hours.

25.—Mistura Bismuthi.

℞   Bismuthi subnitratis...................   gr. v
     Tr. opii deod...........................   ℳ ss
     Syrupi...................................   ℳ x
     Mist. cretæ.................q. s...ad.   f ℨ j
   M.—Dose, f ℨ j, every three or four hours.

26.—Mistura Cretæ Comp.

℞   Tr. opii camphorat...................
     Tr. krameriæ.....................āā...   ℳ v
     Sp. lavandulæ comp...................   ℳ ij
     Misturæ cretæ...............q. s...ad.   f ℨ j
   M.—Dose, f ℨ j, every three or four hours.

27.—Mistura Cretæ et Rhel.

℞ Syr. rhei aromat........................ ℳ xv
   Syr. acaciæ............................. ℳ x
   Misturæ cretæ................q.s...ad. f ʒ j

M.—Dose, f ʒ j, every three or four hours.

28.—Mistura Rhei Comp.

℞ Syr. rhei aromat........................ ℳ xv
   Sodii bicarb............................ gr. ij
   Tr. opii camphorat...................... ℳ v
   Aq. menth. pip..............q. s...ad. f ʒ j

M.—Dose, f ʒ j, every three or four hours.

29.—Mistura Zinci Oxidi.

℞ Zinci oxidi............................. gr. ¼
   Glycerinæ...............................
   Syr. acaciæ........... ....āā... ℳ x
   Aquæ....................….....q. s...ad. f ʒ j

M.—Dose, f ʒ j, every four hours.

Diaphoretic—

30.—Mistura Antifebrilis.

℞ Spt. ætheris nitrosi..............· .....
   Syr. limonis.............…..........…āā... ℳ x
   Liquor ammonii acetat.... .q. s...ad. f ʒ j

M.—Dos.., f ʒ j, every three or four hours.

31.—Mistura Potassii Citratis.

℞ Spt. ætheris nitrosi..................... ℳ x
   Liq. potas. citrat...........q. s...ad. f ʒ j

M.—Dose, f ʒ j, every two or three hours.

32.—Mistura Potassii Citratis Comp.

℞ Potassii citratis...........................   gr. ij ss
    Spt. ætheris nitrosi....................   m x
    Syrupi.....................................   m xx
    Aquæ cinnamomi............q. s...ad.   f ℥ j

M.—Dose, f ℥ j, every two or three hours.

Digestant—

33.—Mistura Pepsinæ.

℞ Pepsinæ saccharat.........,...........   gr. iij
    Acidi muriatici dil....................   m iij
    Glycerinæ...............................   m v
    Aquæ...........................q. s...ad.   f ℥ j

M.—Dose, f ℥ j, three times a day in water, after meals.

Diuretic—

34.—Mistura Digitalis.

℞ Potassii acetatis...... ....   gr. ij ss
    Tincturæ digitalis...... ....   m j ss
    Syr. scillæ...............................   m ij ss
    Syr. zingiberis.........................   m x
    Aquæ..........................q. s...ad.   f ℥ j

M.—Dose, f ℥ j, every two or three hours.

35.—Mistura Ferri Acetatis.

℞ Tinct. ferri chloridi..................   m ij
    Acidi acetici dil......................   m iv
    Liq. ammon. acetatis................   m xl
    Syrupi......................q. s...ad.   f ℥ j

M.—Dose, f ℥ j, three or four times a day.

36.—Mistura Potassii Acetatis.

℞ Potassii acetatis.......................... gr. ij ss
Spt. juniperis comp..................... ℳ v
Spt. ætheris nitrosi..................... ℳ x
Syrupi..................................... ℳ xv
Aquæ.......................q. s...ad. f ℥ j
M.—Dose, f ℥ j, every three or four hours.

Expectorant—

37.—Mist. Ammonii Carbonatis et Senegæ.

℞ Ammonii carbonatis................... gr. j
Syr. tolutani............................. ℳ x
Syr. senegæ.............................. ℳ iij
Mucilag. acaciæ...........q. s...ad. f ℥ j
M.—Dose, f ℥ j, every two or three hours.

38.—Mistura Ammonii Chloridi.

℞ Ammonii chloridi...................... gr. ij
Ext. glycyrrhizæ fld...................
Syrupi...........................āā... ℳ v
Aquæ.......................q. s...ad. f ℥ j
M.—Dose, f ℥ j, every three or four hours.

39.—Mistura Ammonii Chloridi Comp.

℞ Ammonii chloridi...................... gr. ij
Syrupi.....................................
Mist. glycyrrhizæ comp.........āā... f ℥ ss
M.—Dose, f ℥ j, every three or four hours. Shake.

40.—Mistura Ipecacuanhæ Comp.

R Potassii citratis........................... gr. iij
Syrupus ipecacuanhæ.................. ℳ iij
Tr. opii deodorat....................... ℳ ss
Syrupi..................................... ℳ xv
Aquæ...........................q. s...ad. f ʒ j
M.—Dose, f ʒ j, every two or three hours.

———

41.—Mistura Ipecacuanhæ et Scillæ.

R Syr. ipecac...............................
Syr. scillæ.......................āā... ℳ v
Glycerinæ............................... ℳ iv
Mucilag. acaciæ............. q. s...ad. f ʒ j
M.—Dose, f ʒ j, every three hours.

———

42.—Mistura Pruni Virginianæ.

R Acidi sulphurici dil..................... ℳ j
Tinct. opii deodorat.................... ℳ ss
Syr. pruni virginianæ.................. f ʒ ss
Aquæ...........................q. s...ad. f ʒ j
M.—Dose, f ʒ j, every two or three hours.

———

43.—Mistura Scillæ Comp.

R Syr. scillæ................................
Vini ipecacuanhæ................āā... ℳ ij ss
Spt. ætheris nitrosi....................
Tr opii camphoratæ.............āā... ℳ iv
Liquor ammonii acetat......q. s...ad. f ʒ j
M.—Dose, f ʒ j, every three or four hours.

Laxative and Cathartic—
44.—Mistura Aloes et Ferri.

℞ Tr. aloes et myrrhæ.....................   ♏ x
    Ferri sulphatis exsiccat................   gr. 1-6
    Syr. rhei aromat.............q. s...ad.   f ℥ j
M.—Dose, f ℥ j, three times daily.

45.—Mistura Magnesii et Opii.

℞ Magnesii sulphatis................. .....   gr. v
    Tr. opii deodorat........................   ♏ ss
    Syrupi ....   ♏ x
    Aq. menth. pip.............q. s...ad.   f ℥ j
M.—Dose, f ℥ j, every three hours.

46.—Mistura Olei Ricini.

℞ Olei ricini................................
    Glycerinæ......................āā...   f ℥ ss
    Ol. cinnamomi........................   ♏ ⅛
M.—Dose, f ℥ j.

47.—Mistura Podophylli.

℞ Resinæ podophylli.....................   gr. 1-48
    Alcohol....................................   ♏ ij
    Syrupi.......................q. s...ad.   f ℥ j
M.—Dose, f ℥ j, two or three times daily.

48.—Mistura Rhei et Myrrhæ.

℞ Syr. rhei...................................   ♏ xx
    Tr. myrrhæ...............................   ♏ ij
    Syr zingib................................   ♏ x
    Syrupi.......................q. s...ad.   f ℥ j
M.—Dose, f ℥ j, three times daily.

49.—Mistura Sennæ.

℞ Inf. sennæ................................   ♏ xv
    Inf. gentianæ comp.........q. s...ad.   f ℨ j

M.—Dose, f ℨ j, three times daily.

Nervous Sedative—
50.--Mistura Belladonnæ.

℞ Tr. belladonnæ.......................... ♏ ij ss
    Syrupi....................................   ♏ xv
    Aquæ.........................q. s...ad.   f ℨ j

M.—Dose, f ℨ j.

51.—Mistura Chloral. Hydrat.

℞ Chloral. hydrat............................. gr. ij ss
    Syr. tolutani...............................
    Aquæ ....āā...   f ℨ ss

M.—Dose, f ℨ j.

52.—Mist. Chloral. et Potass. Bromidi.

℞ Chloral. hydrat........................... gr. ij
    Potass.' bromidi.......................... gr. v
    Aq. camphoræ............................ f ℨ j

M.—Dose, f ℨ j.

Stimulant—
53.—Mistura Ammonii Carbonatis.

℞ Ammonii carbonatis..................... gr. j
    Syr. acaciæ....... .... ♏ xx
    Aq. menth. pip..............q. s...ad.   f ℨ j

M.—Dose, f ℨ j, every two hours.

54.—Mistura Spiriti Vini Gallici.

R Spiriti vini gallici.......................   ♏ xv
   Syrupi...................................   ♏ x
   Aquæ....................q. s...ad.   f ʒ j

M.—Dose, f ʒ j, every three or four hours.

Tonic—
55.—Mistura Cinchonidiæ Comp.

R Cinchonidiæ sulphatis..................   gr. j
   Acidi muriatici dil......................   ♏ j
   Aquæ...................................   ♏ xxx

Ft. sol. et adde—

   Potassii chloratis.......................   gr. ij ss
   Tinct. ferri chloridi.............. ......   ♏ ij
   Syr. zingiberis................q. s...ad.   f ʒ j

M.—Dose, f ʒ j, four times a day or oftener.

56.—Mistura Ferri et Ammon. Citratis.

R Ferri et. ammon. citratis...............   gr. j
   Tr. gentian. comp............... ......   ♏ x
   Spt. lavand. comp.....................   ♏ v
   Syr. limonis................q. s...ad.   f ʒ j

M.— Dose, f ʒ j, three times a day.

57.—Mistura Ferri Comp.

R Tinct. ferri chloridi...................
   Acidi acetici......................āā...   ♏ ij ss
   Liquor ammonii acetatis..............   ♏ xl
   Potassii chloratis......................   gr. ij ss
   Syr. zingiberis................q. s...ad.   f ʒ j

M.—Dose, f ʒ j, every three or four hours.

58.—Mistura Ferri et Potassii Tartratis.

R   Ferri et potassii tart...................... gr. j ss
     Tinct. gentianæ comp................... ℳ xv
     Spt. lavandulæ comp.................... ℳ v
     Syr. limonis...................q. s...ad. f ʒ j
     M.—Dose, f ʒ j, three times a day.

59.—Mistura Ferri et Quiniæ.

R   Quiniæ sulphatis........................ gr. ꝑꝑ
     Tinct. ferri chloridi.................... ℳ ij
     Syr. zingiberis.......................... ℳ xx
     Aquæ..........................q. s...ad. f ʒ j
     M.—Dose, f ʒ j, three times a day.

60.—Mistura Nucis Vomicæ.

R   Tinct. nucis vomicæ.................... ℳ j
     Tinct. gentianæ comp.................. ℳ v
     Aquæ...................q. s...ad. f ʒ j
     M.—Dose, f ʒ j, three times a day.

61.—Mistura Potassii Chloratis.

R   Potassii chlorat........................... gr. ij
     Acidi muriatici dil...................... ℳ ij
     Mellis.............................. .... f ʒ ss
     Aquæ...........................q. s...ad. f ʒ j
     M.—Dose, f ʒ j. three to five times daily, in water.

PULVERES.

Antacid—
62.—Pulvis Bismuthi et Sodii.

℞ Bismuthi subcarbonatis.................
Sodii bicarbonat...................āā...   gr. j

M. et ft. chart. No. j.—Dose, one powder thrice daily.

63.—Pulv. Ipecac. et Cretæ Præparat.

℞ Pulv. ipecac. comp.....................   gr· ⅓
Cretæ præparatæ.....................   gr. iij

M. et ft. chart No. j.—Dose, one powder every six hours.

Anthelmintic—
64.—Pulvis Santonini.

℞ Santonini................................   gr. ss
Sacchari................................   gr. j ss

M. et ft. chart. No. j.—Dose, one powder morning and evening, the second to be followed by a purge.

Astringent—
65.—Pulvis Bismuthi.

℞ Bismuthi subnitratis...................   gr. j
Sacchari................................   gr. ij

M. et ft. chart. No. j.—Dose, one powder.

66.—Pulvis Bismuthi Comp.

℞ Bismuthi subnitratis...................
Pulv. aromatici.................āā...   gr. j

M. et ft. chart. No. j.—Dose, one powder every four or six hours

67.—Pulvis Bismuthi et Acid. Tannici.

℞ Bismuthi subnitratis...................... gr. j
     Acid. tannici.......................... gr. ss

M. et ft. chart. No. j.—Dose, one powder every six hours.

———

68.—Pulvis Bismuthi et Opii.

℞ Bismuthi subnitratis.................. gr. iij
     Pulv. opii............................ gr. 1-10

M. et ft. chart. No. j.—Dose, one powder every six hours.

———

69.—Pulvis Bismuthi, Ipecac. et Ac. Tannici

℞ Pulv. bismuthi et ac. tannici (No. 67) gr. j ss
     Pulv. ipecac. comp................... gr. ⅓

M. et ft. chart. No. j.—Dose, one powder every six hours.

———

70.—Pulvis Plumbi et Opii.

℞ Plumbi acetat......................... gr. 1-12
     Pulv. ipecac. comp................... gr. ⅓
     Sacchari............................. gr. ij

M. et ft. chart. No. j.—Dose, one powder every six hours.

———

71.—Pulvis Testæ Præparat. et Opii.

℞ Testæ præparatæ...................... gr. iij
     Pulv. ipecac. comp.................. gr. ⅓

M. et ft. chart. No. j.—Dose, one powder every six hours.

Digestant—
72.—Pulvis Bismuthi et Pepsinæ.

℞ Bismuthi subnitratis................................. gr. j
Pepsinæ saccharat................................ gr. ij

M. et ft. chart. No. j.—Dose, one powder three times daily.

73.—Pulvis Pepsinæ et Sodii.

℞ Pepsinæ saccharat............................... gr. ij
Sodii bicarbonatis............................... gr. j

M. et ft. chart. No. j.—Dose, one powder three times daily.

Laxative and Cathartic—
74.—Pulvis Hydrarg. Chlorid. Mit.

℞ Hydrarg. chlorid. mitis................. gr. j
Sacchari alba............................. gr. ij

M. et ft. chart. No. j.—Dose, one powder.

75.- Pulvis Ipecacuanhæ et Rhei.

℞ Pulv. ipecacuanhæ....................... gr. ¼
Pulv. rhei............................... gr. j
Sodii bicarbonatis....................... gr. ij

M. et ft. chart. No. j.—Dose, one powder thrice daily.

76.—Pulvis Rhei et Gentianæ.

℞ Rhei pulv...................................
Gentian. pulv.....................āā... gr. j
Sodii bicarbonatis...................... gr. ij

M. et ft. chart. No. j.—Dose, one powder three times a day.

77.—Pulvis Rhei et Magnesii.

℞   Pulv. rhei.................................   gr.
    Magnesii carbonatis.....................   gr. v
    Pulv. zingiberis.........................   gr. 1-6
M. et ft. chart. No. j.—Dose, one powder thrice daily.

——o——

ENEMATA.

78.—Enema Argenti Nitratis.

℞   Argenti nitratis..........................   gr. ¼
    Bismuthi subnitratis.....................   gr. xx
    Tinct. opii deodorat.....................   ♍ iij
    Mucil. acaciæ...........................   f ℥ j
    Aquæ.......................q. s...ad.   f ℥ ij
M.—Dose, f ℥ ij, injected into bowel twice a day.
Shake well.

79.—Enema Opii.

℞   Tinct. opii........ ....   ♍ iij
    Mucil. acaciæ...........................   f ℥ j
    Aquæ.....................q. s...ad.   f ℥ ij
M.—Dose, f ℥ ij, injected into bowel twice a day.

PREPARATIONS

FOR

EXTERNAL USE.

The various fluid preparations embraced in this list are to be kept and dispensed in *colored* and *roughened* bottles, labeled "*For External Use.*"

GARGARISMATA.

80.—Gargarisma Acidi Tannici.

℞ Acidi tannici............................... ℥ j
Glycerinæ.................................. f℥ j
Aquæ...........................q. s...ad. f℥ j
M.—Sig. f ℥ j, to f ℥ viij of water.

81.—Gargarisma Aluminis.

℞ Pulv. aluminis........................... gr. xv
Acidi muriatici dil................. ... ℳ x
Mellis...................................... f℥ j
Aquæ..........................q. s...ad. f℥ j
M.—Sig. f ℥ j, to f ℥ viij of water.

82.—Gargarisma Potassii Chloratis.

℞ Potassii chloratis........................ gr. xx
Glycerinæ .... f℥ j
Aquæ..........................q. s...ad. f℥ j
M.—Sig. f ℥ j, to f ℥ viij of water.

83.—Gargarisma Potass. Chlorat. et Acidi Carbolici.

℞ Acidi carbolici............................ gr. ij
   Garg. pot. chlor. (No. 82)............ f ℥ j
   M.—Sig. f ℥ j, to f ℥ viij of water.

84.—Gargarisma Potass. Chlorat. et Ferri.

℞ Tinct. ferri chloridi....................
   Acidi muriatici dil...............āā... ℳ x
   Garg. pot. chlor. (No. 82)..q. s...ad. f ℥ j
   M.—Sig. f ℥ j, to f ℥ viij of water.

85.—Gargarisma Sodii Boratis.

℞ Sodii boratis............................ gr. xv
   Glycerinæ .... f ℥ ij
   Aquæ..................q. s...ad. f ℥ j
   M.—Sig. f ℥ j, to f ℥ viij of water.

—o—

GLYCERITA.

86.—Glyceritum Iodinii.

℞ Iodinii................................. gr. v
   Glycerinæ..................q. s...ad. f ℥ j
   M.

87.—Glyceritum Tr. Ferri Chloridi.

℞ Tr. ferri chloridi...................... f ℥ j
   Glycerinæ..................q. s...ad. f ℥ j
   M.

LINIMENTA.

88.—Linimentum Aconiti Comp.

℞ Tinct. aconiti radicis.................
Chloroformi.............. ....āā...   ℥ xv
Liniment. saponis............q. s...ad.   f℥ j
M.

89.—Linimentum Ol. Succini.

℞ Ol. succini...............................
Ol. olivæ.........................āā...   f℥ ss
M.

90.—Linimentum Sapon. Viridis.

℞ Saponis viridis..........................   ℥ j
Alcoholis..............................   f℥ j
M.

——o——

LIQUORES.

91.—Liquor Acidi Boracici.

℞ Acidi boracici...........................   gr. xv
Aquæ destillatæ.......................   f℥ j
M.

92.—Liquor Acidi Tannici.

℞ Acidi tannici...........................   gr. viij
Aquæ destillatæ.......................   f℥ j
M.

93.—Liquor Aluminis.

℞ Aluminis .... gr. iv
   Aquæ rosæ............................... f ℥ j
M.

94.—Liquor Argenti Nitratis.

℞ Argenti nitratis......................... gr. ss
   Aquæ destillatæ......................... f ℥ j
M.

95.—Liquor Atropiæ.

℞ Atropiæ sulphatis....................... gr. iv
   Aquæ destillatæ......................... f ℥ j
M.

96.—Liquor Hydrargyri.

℞ Hydrarg. chloridi corrosivi........... gr. 1-ʄ
   Aquæ destillatæ......................... f ℥ j
M.

97.—Liquor Plumbi Subacetatis.

℞ Liquor plumbi subacetatis............ ℳ xv
   Aquæ destillatæ.............q. s...ad. f ℥ j
M.

98.—Liquor Sodii Boratis.

℞ Sodii boratis............................. gr. x
   Aquæ destillatæ......................... f ℥ j
M.

LOTIONES.

99.—Lotio Acidi Sulphurosi.

℞ Acidi sulphurosi........................ f ℥ ij ss
Aquæ............... ....q. s...ad. f ℥ j
M.

100.—Lotio Cocculi Indici.

℞ Tinct. cocculi indici....................
Alcoholis...........................āā... f ℥ ss
M.—Sig. To be diluted.

101.—Lotio Sodii Hyposulphitis.

℞ Sodii hyposulphitis.................... ℥ ij
Aquæ destillatæ...................... f ℥ j
M.

UNGUENTA.

102.—Unguentum Hydrarg. Ammoniati Dil.

℞ Ung. hydrarg. ammoniat..............
Adipis ....āā... ℥ ss
M.

103.—Unguentum Hydrargyri Nitrat. Dil.

℞ Ung. hydrarg. nitrat................... ℥ j
Adipis...................................... ℥ vij
M.

104.—Ung. Hydrarg. Oxidi Flav. Dil.

℞ Hydrarg. oxidi flav...................... gr. viij
   Ung. petrolei........................... ℥ j
M.

105.—Unguentum Hydrarg. Oxidi Rub. Dil.

℞ Ung. hydrarg. oxid. rub.............. ℥ j
   Adipis .... ℥ vij
M.

106.—Unguentum Hydrargyri et Belladonnæ

℞ Ext. belladonnæ....................... ℥ iij
   Ung. hydrargyri....................... ℥ v
   Ol. amygdal............................. ♏ xv
M.

107.—Unguentum Picis Liquidæ Dil.

℞ Ung. picis liquidæ....................
   Adipis............................āā... ℥ ss
M.

108.—Unguentum Plumbi Subacetatis Dil.

℞ Cerat. plumbi subacetat.............. ℥ j
   Glycerinæ............................... f℥ ij
   Adipis.................................... ℥ v
M.

109.—Unguentum Sulphuris et Potass. Carb.

℞ Potassii carbonatis..................... ℥ j
   Ung. sulphuris......................... ℥ ij
   Adipis .... ℥ vj
M.

APPENDIX:

Containing those preparations of the U. S. Pharmacopœia most commonly employed in Children's Diseases, together with their doses for Children two years old.

Aceta—

Acetum opii........................	℥	ss–j
" scillæ........................	℥	j–v

Acida—

Acidum aceticum dil................	℥	xv–v
" carbolicum	gr.	⅛
" gallicum	gr.	ss–ij
" hydrocyanicum dil..........	℥	⅛–¼
" muriaticum dil.............	℥	j–v
" nitricum dil...............	℥	j–iij
" nitromuriaticum dil........	℥	j–v
" phosphoricum dil..........	℥	j–v
" salicylicum	gr.	j
" sulphuricum dil............	℥	j–v
" " aromat.........	℥	j–v
" tannicum.................	gr.	ss–ij

Ætherea—

Æther	℥	ij–x
Chloroformum....................	℥	j–v

Ammonia—

Ammonii bromidum................	gr.	j–v
" carbonas	gr.	ss–j
" chloridum...............	gr.	j–v

Acid. nitric. dil............................   O j
  "   muriatic. dil..........................   O ij

M.

Antimonium—

Antimonii et potassii tartras...........   gr. 1-48–¼

Aquæ—

Aquæ ammoniæ (External)...........
  "   camphoræ.........................   f ʒ j
  "   cinnamomi.........................   f ʒ j–ij
  "   menthæ piperitæ...............   f ʒ j–ij
  "   rosæ (External)..................

Argentum—

Argenti nitras............................   gr. 1-64–1-32
  "   "   fusa (External).......

Bismuthum—

Bismuthi subcarbonas..................   gr. j–v
  "   subnitras......................   gr. j–v

Calcium—

Calcii lactophosphatum...............   gr. j–ij
Creta præparata.........................   gr. ij-x
Testa   "   ....   gr. ij–x

Cerata (External)—

Ceratum canth.	Ceratum resinæ comp.
" cetacei.	" sabinæ.
" ext. canth.	" saponis.
" plumbi sub.	" zinci carbon.
" resinæ.	

Chartæ (External)—

Charta cantharidis.
" sinapis.

Collodium (External)—

Collodium cum cantharide.
Collodium flexile.

Confectiones—

Confectio sennæ........................ gr. x–xx

Decocta—

Decoctum dulcamaræ................. f ℥ j–ij
" hæmatoxyli.................. f ℥ j–ij
" hordei ....ı............... f ℥ j–iv
" quercus albæ (External)...
" uvæ ursi..................... f ℥ j–ij

Emplastra (External)—

Emplastrum assafœtidæ.
" belladonnæ.
" hydrargyri.
" opii.
" picis burgundicæ.
" " cum cantharide.
" " resinæ.
" " saponis.

Extracta—

Extractum	belladonnæ.................	gr. 1-32–1-16
"	cinchonæ.....................	gr. j–iv
"	colocynthidis c............	gr. ¼–j
"	gentianæ.....................	gI. ss–j
"	glycyrrhizæ	gr. j–v
"	hæmatoxyli	gr. j–iv
"	hyoscyami..................	gr. 1-16–¼
"	krameriæ....................	gr. ss–ij
"	nucis vomicæ..............	gr. 1-48–1-24
"	taraxaci......	gr. ij–x

Extracta Fluida—

Extractum	buchu fluid.................	♏ ij–v
"	cimicifugæ fluid...........	♏ iv–viij
"	ergotæ fluid................	♏ j–ij
"	jaborandi fluid.............	♏ x
"	pruni virg. fluid...........	♏ x
"	rhei fluid....................	♏ j–v
"	sennæ fluid.................	♏ x–xxx
"	spigeliæ et sen. fluid......	f ℥ j
"	uvæ ursi fluid..............	♏ ij–v
"	valerianæ fluid.............	♏ ij–x

Ferrum—

Ferri	citras...............................	gr. ss–ij
"	et ammonii citras..............	gr. ss–ij
"	et potassii tartras..............	gr. ss–ij
"	et quiniæ citras................	gr. ss–ij
"	lactas.............................	gr. ss–ij
"	pyrophosphas...................	gr. ¼–j
"	subcarbonas....................	gr. j–ij
"	sulphas exsiccata..............	gr. ¼–j
Ferrum redactum......................		gr. ss–ij

Glycerita (External)—

Glyceritum acidi carbolici.
" " gallici.
" " tannici.
" picis liquidæ.
" sodii boratis.

Hydrargyrum—

Hydrargyri chloridum corros........... gr. 1-100–1-32
" " mite............ gr. 1-24–ss
Hydrargyrum cum creta............... gr. ss–jss

Infusa—

Infusum buchu........................ f ℥ j–ij
" calumbæ.................... f ℥ j–ij
" digitalis..................... m x–f ℥ ss
" gentianæ comp.............. f ℥ ss–j
" jaborandi.................... f ℥ j–ij
" juniperi .... f ℥ j–ij
" lini comp.................... f ℥ ss–ij
" sennæ....................... f ℥ ss–j
" spigeliæ..................... f ℥ j–ij

Linimenta (External)—

Linimentum aconiti.
" ammoniæ.
" calcis.
" camphoræ.
" cantharidis.
" chloroformi.
" plumbi subacetatis.
" saponis
" terebinthinæ

Liquores—

Liquor ammonii acetatis................	f ℥ ss–j
" arsenici chloridi................	♏ j–iij
" arsenici et hydrarg. iodidi...	♏ ss–j
" calcis....................	f ℥ j–f ℥ iij
" ferri nitratis....................	♏ j–iij
" " subsulphatis..............	♏ ss–j
" magnesii citratis................	f ℥ ij–f ℥ ss
" morphiæ sulphatis..............	♏ ij–x
" potassii arsenitis..............	♏ j–iij
" " citratis................	f ℥ ss–j

Magnesium—

Magnesia................................	gr. v–Ɔ ij
Magnesii carbonas......................	gr. v–Ɔ ij

Manna—...................................... gr. xx–ʒ j

Mellita (External)—

Mel despumatum.
" rosæ.
" sodii boratis.

Misturæ—

Mistura ammoniaci....................	f ℥ ss–ij
" amygdalæ......................	f ℥ j–f ℥ j
" assafœtidæ......................	f ℥ j–ij
" chloroformi	f ℥ j–ij
" cretæ............................	f ℥ ss–j
" ferri comp......................	f ℥ j–ij
" glycyrrhizæ comp............	♏ xv–f ℥ ss
" potassii citratis................	f ℥ ss–j

Morphia—

Morphiæ acetas	gr.	1-48–1-30
" murias	gr.	1-48–1-30
" sulphas	gr.	1-48–1-30

Mucilagines—

Mucilago acaciæ	ad lib.
" sassafras medullæ	ad lib.
" tragacanthæ	ad lib.
" ulmi	ad lib.

Olea—

Oleum chenopodii	ℳ ij–iv
" menthæ piperitæ	ℳ ss–j
" morrhuæ	ℳ xv–f ℥ j
" olivæ	f ℥ ji–j
" ricini	f ℥ ss–ij
" terebinthinæ	ℳ ij–v

Oleoresinæ—

Oleoresina filicis	ℳ v–xx

Opium— gr. 1-10–1·8

Pepo— ℥ j–ij

Phosphorus— gr. 1-160 1-100

Plumbum—

Plumbi acetas	gr.	1.8–1-6

Potassium —

Potassii acetas	gr. ij–v
" bicarbonas	gr. ij–v
" bitartras	gr. x–xv
" bromidum	gr. ij–v
" chloras	gr. ij–v
" citras	gr. ij–v
" et sodii tartras	gr. xv–ℨ j
" iodidum	gr. ss–iij
" nitras	gr. jss–viij

Pulveres—

Pulvis aromaticus	gr. j–ij
" ipecacuanhæ comp	gr. ¼–jss

Quinia—

Quiniæ sulphas	gr. ss–iv
" valerianas	gr. ¼–ss

Resinæ—

Resina jalapæ	gr. ¼–ss
" podophylli	gr. 1-64–1.45
" scammonii	gr. ¼–jss

Rheum— gr. ss–ij

Rettlera (Kameela)— gr. v–xv

Santoninum— gr. ¼–ss

Scammonium— gr. j–ij

Senna— gr. iij–v

Sinapis (Emetic)—...................... gr. viij–xx

Sodium—

Sodii acetas............................ gr. ij–v
"   arsenias .... gr 1-160–1-64
"   bicarbonas........................ gr. ij–v

Spiritus—

Spiritus ætheris comp.................. ℥ ij–x
"   "   nitrosi............... ℥ v–xx
"   ammoniæ aromat............. ℥ ij–v
"   camphoræ..................... ℥ ss–iv
"   chloroformi................... ℥ j–v
"   cinnamomi.................... ℥ j–ij
"   frumenti....................... ℥ v–f℥ j
"   juniperi comp................ ℥ v–xv
"   lavandulæ comp............. ℥ v–xx
"   menthæ piperitæ............. ℥ ss–ij
"   vini gallici.................... ℥ v–f℥ j

Strychnia—

Strychniæ sulphas................... gr. 1-150–1-100

Sulphur—

Sulphur præcipitatum................ gr. v–xv

Syrupi—

Syrupus acaciæ........................	ad lib.
"	ferri iodidi.....................	♏ ij–v
"	ipecacuanhæ	♏ ij–f ʒ j
"	krameriæ.......................	♏ xx–f ʒ j
"	lactucarii.......................	♏ xx–f ʒ j
"	limonis	ad lib.
"	pruni virginianæ.............	♏ xv–f ʒ ss
"	rhei..............................	f ʒ ss–j
"	" aromat...................	f ʒ ss–j
"	sarsaparillæ comp............	♏ xv–f ʒ ss
"	scillæ...........................	♏ ij–vj
"	" comp	♏ ij–vj
"	tolutani	♏ ij–vj
"	zingiberis......................	♏ v–x

Tincturæ—

Tinctura belladonnæ..................	♏ j–ij
"	calumbæ	♏ iij–xv
"	cannabis.......................	♏ j–ij
"	cardamomi comp...........	♏ v–xv
"	catechu........................	♏ v–xv
"	cinchonæ comp..............	♏ x–xv
"	cinnamomi.............	♏ ij–xv
"	colchici........................	♏ j–iij
"	digitalis......................	♏ ss–iij
"	ferri chloridi	♏ j–v
"	gentianæ comp...............	♏ v–xv
"	guaiaci ammon...............	♏ v–xv
"	hyoscyami	♏ j–iv
"	iodinii comp..................	♏ j–iv
"	kino.............................	♏ ij–xx
"	krameriæ......................	♏ ij–xx
"	nucis vomicæ................	♏ ss–ij

Tinctura opii............................ ♏ j–iij
" " camphorata........... .... ♏ v–xx
" " deodorata............... ♏ j–iij
" scillæ........................... ♏ j–v
" valerianæ ammoniata...... ♏ v–xv
" zingiberis .... ♏ ij–vij

Unguenta (External)—

Unguentum acidi carbolici.
" " tannici.
" aquæ rosæ.
" belladonnæ.
" benzoini.
" cantharidis.
" creasoti.
" gallæ.
" hydrargyri.
" " ammoniati.
" " iodidi rubri.
" " nitratis.
" " oxidi flavi.
" " " rubri.
" iodinii.
" " compositum.
" mezerei.
" picis liquidæ.
" plumbi carbonatis.
" " iodidi.
" potassii iodidi.
" stramonii.
" sulphuris.
" " iodidi.
" veratriæ.
" zinci oxidi.

Vina—

Vinum ergotæ............................	℥	v–x
" ipecacuanhæ....................	gtt.	ij–viij
" opii............................	℥	ss–j
" rhei.............................	℥	v–f ℨ ss
" xericum......	℥	x–f ℨ j
" portense...........................	℥	v–f ℨ j

Zincum—

Zinci oxidum............................	gr.	⅛–ss
" sulphas............................	gr.	⅛–v
" valerianas.........................	gr.	⅛–ss

Zingiber—

Pulv. zingiberis...........................	gr.	1-6-ij

NON-OFFICINAL REMEDIES.

Acidum salicylicum....................	gr.	ss–iss
Pepsina saccharata.....................	gr.	j–v
Pulv. glycyrrhizæ comp...............	gr.	iv–viij
Sodii bromidum........................	gr.	j–v
Sodii salicylas	gr.	ss–j ss

POISONS AND THEIR ANTIDOTES.

Acids, Mineral.—Alkalies in dilute solution; lime; whitewash; magnesia; soap.
Quickness of administration essential.
Avoid emetics and stomach-pump.

Acids, Vegetable—Soap; soda or potassa in dilute solution; except for *oxalic acid*, for which give lime, whitewash, or chalk.

Aconite.—Emetics; stomach-pump; tannic acid; digitalis; laudanum; warmth; stimulation; recumbent position.

Alkalies, and their salts.—Vinegar; weak acids; oil, freely; opium.

Alum.—Albumen.

Antimony, and its salts.—Tannic acid; opium; external warmth.

Arsenic, and its salts.—Emetics; stomach-pump; recently made hydrated sesquioxide of iron; magnesia; dialysed iron; oil or fat.

Atropia.—See Belladonna.

Belladonna.—Emetics; stomach-pump; tannic acid; morphia hypodermically.

Bismuth, and its compounds.—Albumen; milk.

Bromine.—Soap; oils.

Cannabis Indica.—Emetics; lemon juice; quiet; if exhaustion, stimulants.

Carbolic Acid.—Stomach-pump; solution of saccharate of lime; hot and cold douche.

Chloral and Chloroform.—Alternate hot and cold douche; artificial respiration; cardiac stimulants

Cocculus Indicus.—Emetics; stomach-pump; at first, give opium; chloral; chloroform; later, stimulants. No chemical antidote.

Colchicum.—Emetics; stomach-pump; tannic acid; opium; stimulants.

Conium.—Emetics; stomach-pump; artificial respiration; tannic acid; opium.

Copper, and its salts.—Albumen; milk; calcined mag nesia; yellow prussiate of potash.

Croton Oil, and other drastic purgatives.—Emetics; albuminous drinks; bismuth; external heat.

Cyanide of potassium.—See Hydrocyanic acid.

Digitalis—Emetics; stomach-pump; tannic acid; stim ulants.

Gelsemium.—Same as Aconite.

Hydrocyanic acid.—Alternate hot and cold douche; intravenous injection of aqua ammoniæ; atropia hypodermically.

Hyoscyamus.—Same as Belladonna.

Iodine.—Starch, freely; if this cannot be obtained, then soap.

Iron, Salts of—Soap; dilute alkalies; albumen.

Lead, Salts of—Emetics; stomach-pump; alkaline sulphates; soap; albumen; milk; purge.

Mercury, Salts of—Emetics; albumen; milk.

Opium.—Stomach-pump; atropia hypodermically; coffee; flagellation; artificial respiration; electricity.

Phosphorus.—Emetics; sulphate of copper in small doses; crude oil of turpentine; stomach-pump; avoid oils or fats.

Potash Salts.—No distinct antidote.

Santonin.—Emetics; purges; stimulants; artificial respiration.

Silver, Salts of—Common salt, freely; albumen.

Soda Salts.—No distinet antidote.

Stramonium.—Same as Belladonna.

Strychnia.—Emetics ; stomach-pump (*at first* only) ; tannic acid ; chloral ; bromide of potash ; ether ; chloroform ; rest.

Veratrum viride.—Same as Aconite.

Zinc, Salts of—Albumen ; carbonate of soda ; milk, freely.

——o——

INFANT DIET.

Diet from Birth to Age of Six Months.

(Five to six meals in 24 hours.)

MILK, CREAM, LIME-WATER, ARROWROOT WATER.

Take four tablespoonfuls of each, place in bottle with a lump of sugar, warm the whole by standing bottle in warm water.

Arrowroot Water is made by taking *one and a half teaspoonfuls* of arrowroot, rubbing it down until smooth, with a tablespoonful of cold water, and then adding *one pint* of boiling water, stirring all the time.

Diet from Six to Twelve Months Old.

(Five meals in the day.)

FIRST MEAL, 7 A. M.

Mellin's food, one tablespoonful, or Flonr Ball grated, one or two teaspoonfuls.

Hot water, four tablespoonfuls.

Warm milk, enough to make half a pint.

Dissolve the Mellin's food or rub down the grated Flour Ball in the hot water by stirring, then add the milk, and mix thoroughly.

SECOND MEAL, 10.30 A. M.   THIRD MEAL. 2 P. M.
 A breakfast cupful of milk with four tablespoonfuls
of lime-water,
FOURTH MEAL, 5.30 P. M.   Same as first.
FIFTH MEAL, 10.30 P. M.   Same as second.

Diet for a Child One Year Old.

(Five meals in the day.)

FIRST MEAL, 7 A. M.
 Two teaspoonfuls of grated Flour Ball in half a pint
of milk.
SECOND MEAL, 10.30 A. M.
 Half a pint of milk with four tablespoonfuls of lime-
water.
THIRD MEAL, 2 P. M.
 The yolk of one egg beaten up in a teacupful of
milk.
FOURTH MEAL, 5.30 P. M.   Same as the first.
FIFTH MEAL.   Same as the second.
FOR DRINK—Filtered water.

Diet for a Child Two Years Old.

BREAKFAST, 7.30 A. M.
 Milk.
 The lightly boiled yolk of an egg.
 Thin bread and butter (bread one day old).
LUNCH, 11 A. M.
 Milk.
 A thin slice of bread and butter.
DINNER, 1.30 P. M.
 Beef-tea, or small piece of minced roast beef or
mutton.   One well-mashed potato, moistened with
gravy.
 Rice and milk.

SUPPER, 6 P. M.

Milk.

Bread and butter.

FOR DRINK—Filtered water.

Diet in Mucous Disease for a Child of Seven Years.

BREAKFAST, 7.30 A. M.

Milk, with lime water; four tablespoonfuls of lime-water to each tumblerful of milk.

The lightly-boiled yolk of an egg, a thin slice of well-toasted bread, or stale bread.

DINNER, 12 M.

A mutton chop without fat, broiled, or a slice of roast beef or mutton, occasionally a bowl of meat broth. Stale bread or toast.

SUPPER, 7 P. M.

Milk and lime-water.

Stale bread or toast.

FOR DRINK—Filtered water.

Starch food to be avoided as much as possible.

—o—

BARLEY WATER.

To prepare barley water, put two good teaspoonfuls of washed pearl barley with a pint of cold water in a saucepan, and boil slowly down to two-thirds. Strain.

BEEF-TEA.

Take one pound of lean beef, and mince it. Put it, with its juice, into an *earthen* vessel containing a pint of *tepid water*, and let the whole stand for one hour; strain well, squeezing all the juice from the meat Place on the fire, and slowly raise *just to the boiling point, stirring it briskly* all the time. Season with salt and pepper to taste.

In administering this, always be careful to stir up the sediment.

FLOUR BALL.

Take one pound of good flour—unbolted, if possible —tie it up *very tightly* in a pudding-bag; put it in a pot of boiling water early in the morning, and let it boil till bed time, then take it out and let it dry. In the morning peel off from the surface, and throw away, the thin rind of dough, and with a grater, grate down the hard dry mass into a powder. To use this, take from one to two teaspoonfuls of the powder, rub it down till smooth with a tablespoonful of cold milk, and add a tumblerful of hot milk, stirring it well all the time.

LIME-WATER.

Take a piece of unslacked lime, as large as a walnut, put it into two quarts of clear water, stir about thoroughly, allow to settle, and use only from the top.

WINE WHEY.

Boil in a pint of fresh milk; while boiling, pour in a small tumblerful of sherry wine (eight tablespoofuls), bring it to the boil a second time, being careful not to stir it; as soon as it boils set it aside until the curd settles, and pour off the clear whey.

PENNSYLVANIA HOSPITAL
OF
PHILADELPHIA.

St. John Long's Liniment.

Take of—

Yolks of eight eggs.....................		
Spt of turpentine	oz.	24
Acetic acid..............................	oz.	16
Water..................................	oz.	24

Mix.

For Coughs.

Take of—

Brown mixture (officinal)..............	oz.	1
Muriate of ammonia	gr.	10

Mix.—Dose, tablespoonful.

Solution Bromide of Potassium.

℞

Brom. potass...........................	℈	ij
Aquæ..................................	℥	j

M.—Sig. Dose, tablespoonful.

Lead-Water and Laudanum.

Take of—

Laudanum	oz.	4
Goulard's extract........................	oz.	4
Water, to make one-half gallon.		

Mix.

Solutions of Carbolic Acid.

2 per cent., 2½ per cent., 4 per cent. and 5 per cent.

(To make two per cent. solution, add a *little* water to crystals and heat to make it liquid, and put one ounce of acid (by measure) to fifty ounces of water. To render crystals liquid, set bottle in hot water; then add a little water to keep it liquid.)

Solution of Boracic Acid.

℞ Acid. boracici............................ gr. xv
    Aquæ puræ............................ ℥ j

M.—Used mostly for sore eyes.

Carbolized Oil.

Take of—

Calvert's carbolic acid, No. 4........	oz.	1
Olive oil..............	oz.	15

Mix.

Aperient Pills.

℞ Ex. colocynth comp.................... gr. xxiv.
    Ex. nucis vom........................... gr. iij
    Ex. belladonnæ.......................... gr. j

M.—Ft. pil. No. xij.—Sig. One or two.

Niemeyer's Pills.

℞ Quiniæ sulph............................. gr. xij
    Pulv. digitalis........................... gr. vj
    Pulv. opii................................ gr. iij
  M.—Ft. pil. No. xij.—Sig. One, three times a day.

Diarrhœa Mixture.

Take of—
    Chalk mixture........................... oz. 4
    Paregoric................................ oz. 2
    Tr. catechu............................. oz. 2
  Mix.—Dose, two teaspoonfuls.

Chlorate of Patassa Solution.

℞ Potass. chlor............................. gr. xxx.
    Aquæ.................................... $\mathrecipe{3}$ j
  Dissolve. For throat trouble.

Compound Gentian Mixture.

℞ Ferri cit. et ammon..................... ℈ ij
    Fl. ex. gentian......................... ʒ vj
    Spt. lavand. comp...................... O j
    Alcoholis............................... O ss
    Syrup. simp............................. ℥ xxiv
    Aquæ..........................ad... C j
  M.—Use as a tonic.

Basham's Mixture.

℞ Sal. ammon. acet........................ ℥ xxx
  Acid. acet............................... ℥ xv
  Tr. ferri chlor........................... ℥ xxv
  Alcoholis................................ ℥ x
  Syr. simplicis........................... ℥ xx
  Aquæ.................................... ℥ xv

M. – Dose, tablespoonful three times a day.

(Note.—It will be noticed that the proportion of alcohol in the above is greater than in the officinal formula. This makes it keep better in a warm place.)

Solution Iodidi Potass.

℞ Potass iodidi........................... ℈ j
  Aquæ cinnam.........................
  Aquæ.......................āā... ℥ ss

M.—Dose, tablespoonful. Sometimes we use solution double strength.

Solution Quinæ.

℞ Sul. quiniæ............................. ℨ ij ℥ j gr. iv
  Acid sulph. c. p....................... ♏ lxxx
  Aquæ .... one gallon

Put quinine in mortar, add half pint water, add acid and dissolve, then add remainder of water. This gives a solution of one grain to the ounce.

JEFFERSON COLLEGE HOSPITAL

OF

PHILADELPHIA.

Iodoform Cotton.

Take of—

Cotton..	gr. 70
Glycerine.......................................minims	10
Alcohol, (sp. gr. 796)...................	dr. 2
Ether, (sp. gr. 730).....................	oz. 1, or suffict.
Iodoform .... ·	dr. 1

Mix.—Dissolve the iodoform in the ether, add the giycerine, mixed with the alcohol; saturate the cotton with the above mixture, and dry by exposure.

Koumys.

Take of—

Sugar......................................	dr. 6
Compressed yeast, (very fresh, size of pea).	

Mix.—Fresh milk, to fill champagne bottle. Cork tightly; keep in temperature of about 80°, first twenty-four hours, and shake occasionally; then keep in cool place (on ice) two days.

Catarrh Powder—(Sajou's).

℞   Morphiæ muriat........................   gr. ss
      Pulv. acaciæ...............................   gr. xxx
      Bismuth sub-nit.........................   ℥ iss
      Pulv. talc.................................   ℥ j
M.—Sig. Insufflate.

Pancoast's Pill of Hydrarg. Comp.

℞   Mass. hydrarg...........................   gr. j
      Ex. jalapæ................................   gr. ss
      Ex. colocynthis comp..................   gr. ij
      Ol. menth. pip...........................   gtt. ss
   M.—Make one pill.   Sig. One at night.

S. W. Gross' Fever Mixture.

℞   Liq. potassii citratis....................   ℥ ss
      (or liq. ammonii acetatis ℥ ss).
      Spts. ætheris nitrosi.....................   ℥ j
      Tinct. aconiti rad.......................   gtt. ij
      Morphiæ sulphat........................   gr. 1-16
   M.—Sig. To be taken every three, four or five hours.

Ergotine Solution for Hypodermic Use.

℞   Ergotine...................................   gr. xl
      Glycerini..................................   ℳ xxx
      Aquæ......................................   gr. ℥ ij
   M. ft. sol.   Ten minims contain four grains of ergotine.

S. D. Gross' Antimony and Saline Mixture.

R Antimonii et potass. tart............... gr. ij ss
   Magnesii sulphat........................ ℥ ij
   Morphiæ sulphat........................ gr. i⅓
   Aquæ dest.............................. ℥ x
   Syr. zingiberis .... ℥ ij
   Tr. verat viridi vel aconiti............. ℥ j ss

M.—Sig. Tablespoonful every two, three, four or six hours. Used in acute stages of gonorrhœa and other inflammations.

Sajou's Douche.

(For Nasal Catarrh.)

Sodii salicylici........................... ℥ x
Sodii biborat............................. ℥ xv
Glycerini................................. ℥ ij ss
Aquæ..................................... ℥ xxx

M.—Sig. Use as a douche or spray morning and night.

Parvin's Carcinoma Solution.

R Iodinii .... ℥ j.
   Brominii................................ ℥ ꝯ
   Acid. carbolici......................... ℥ iv
   Alcoholis............................... ℥ j

M.—Apply to parts, and follow with saturated solution of bicarbonate of soda, to neutralize any excess. To be used to destroy diseased tissue not removed by operation.

Unguentum Boro-Glyceride.

R Boro-glyceride (50 per cent)......... ℥ j
   Ung. petrolei............................ ℥ v
Mix with gentle heat.

Used in conjunctivitis, and ulcerated cornea. May be used in ulcerated conditions in any part of the body.

Boro-Glyceride.

Take of—

Glycerine (50 per cent. solution)....   gr. 92
Boracic acid.........................   gr. 62

Stir with gentle heat until mixture crystalizes upon cooling; then add, while warm, 50 per cent. of glycerine by weight. This can be diluted with water to any desired strength. Used extensively here, in 25 per cent. solution, for catarrh of nasal and pharyngeal membranes.

Mist. Guaiaci Comp.

(For Throat Troubles.)

℞   Tr. guaiaci ammon................
Tr. cinchon. comp..............āā ..   ℥ ij
Potass. chlorat....................   ℥ j
Mel. despumat.....................   ℥ vj
Aquæ.....................q. s...   ℥ iij

M.—Sig. To be used as a gargle and swallowed.

Lupulin Mixture.

(Diuretic.)

℞   Lupulinæ........................   ℥ ij
Uvæ ursi.......................   ℥ ij
Sodæ bi-carb...................   ℥ ss
Tr. opii camph.................   ℥ iv
Aquæ.....................q. s...   O ij

Make decoction of lupulin and uva ursi and add other ingredients. Dose, tablespoonful three times a day.

Da Costa's Solution of Quinine for Hypodermic Use.

℞ Quiniæ sulph............................. gr. xl
　Sol. acid. tart. sat....................... ℳ xlviij
　Aquæ...........................q. s... ℥ ij

M.—Dose according to requirements.

Hughes' Rhubarb Mixture.

(For Dyspepsia.)

℞ Sodii bicarb............................. ℥ v
　Tr. nucis vom................ .... ℥ iij ℥ vj
　Tr. capsici.............................. ℥ ij ℥ ij
　Tr. rhei................................... ℥ xx
　Tr. gentian comp.............. .. ℥ xx

M.—One to two teaspoonfuls after meals.

FORMULARY

OF THE

NEW YORK HOSPITAL.
(NEW YORK CITY.)

FOR EXTERNAL USE.

Antiseptic Solutions.

Sol. carbolic acid........................	1–20	water
" " "	1–30	"
" " "	1–40	"
" boracic "	1–30	"
" thymol.............................	1–1000	"

Distilled water is preferred; it will make a clearer solution than ordinary water.

White Wash.

℞   Potassii sulphuret........................
Zinci sulphat......................āā...   ℥ j
Aquæ...   ℥ iv

Dissolve each in two ounces of water and mix.

Carbolic Throat Spray.

℞ Sodii bicarb............................
    Sodii biborat.....................āā... ℥ j
    Acidi carbolici.......................... gr. xl
    Glycerinæ.............................. ℥ vij
    Aquæ.....................ad... ℥ viij
   M.

Red Wash.

℞ Zinci sulphat............................ ℈ ij
    Spt. lavand. comp .... f℥ j
    Aquæ...................................... O j
    Cochineal coloring.................... q. s.
   M.

Ward Gargle.

℞ Tannin................................... ℥ ss
    Sol. potassii chlorat. sat.............. ℥ viij
   M.

Muriate of Ammonia Wash.

℞ Ammonii chloridi....................... ℥ ss
    Tinct. opii............................... ℥ j
    Aquæ.....................ad... O ij
   M.

Lead and Opium Wash.

℞ Liquor plumbi subacet................. ℥ iij
    Aquæ...................................... O j
    Tr. opii.................................... ℥ iv
   M.

Alkaline Tar Water.

℞ Picis liquidæ.............................. ℥ ij
    Potassæ causticæ....................... ℥ j
    Aquæ .... ℥ v
M.

Compound Tincture of Green Soap.

Take of—
    Oil of cade..............................
    Green soap...............................
    Alcohol .... equal parts.
M.

Churchill's Tincture of Iodine.

℞ Iodinii .... ℥ j
    Potassii iodidi........................... ℥ ij
    Aquæ destil...............................
    Alcoholis..........................āā... f℥ ij

Iodoform Cylinders.

℞ Iodoformi .... ℥ ij ss
    Tragacanth................... .... gr. xv
    Mucilag. acaciæ....................... q. s.
Divide into 10 cylinders, 1 ½ in. long.

Parasiticide.

℞ Acidi carbol.............................. gr. x
    Ung. hydrarg. nitrat..................
    Sulphur. precip....................āā... ℥ j
    Ung. simplicis .... ℥ j

Epilating Stick.

Take of—

Wax..................................	℥	iij
Shellac.............................	℥	iv
Rosin	℥	vj
Burgundy pitch.....................	℥	x
Damar	℥	xij

Melt together and roll into sticks of different diameters.

Colorless Evaporating Lotion.

℞

Ammon. hydrochlor...............	gr.	xij
Spt. vini rect	♏	xxxiv
Aquæ..............................	℥	j

Lotion of Calamine and Zinc Oxide.

℞

Pulv. calamin. prep...............			
Zinci oxidi.................. āā...	℥	j	
Glycerinæ........................	℥	ij	
Aquæ	℥	iv	

Stimulating Lotion.

℞

Arnicæ tinct......................	♏	xx
Spt. rosmarin	♏	xv
Aq. dest..........................	℥	j

OINTMENTS.

Carbolized Cosmoline (Saturated.)

℞   Cosmolinæ ....   ℥ xx
     Acid. carbolici crystal..................   ℥ j
  Melt each separately and mix.

Ointment of Chrysophanic Acid, Concentrated.

℞   Acid. chrysophanic.....................   ℥ j
     Ung. simplicis..........................   ℥ iv
  Melt the ointment, and while hot add the acid, stirring
till dissolved.

Brown Ointment.

℞   Pulv. acid. salicylici ....   gr. xl
     Bals. Peruvian...........................   ℥ j
     Cosmolinæ................................   ℥ j

Ointment of Salicylic Acid.

℞   Pulv. acid. salicylici....................   ℥ j
     Cosmolinæ..............................   ℥ j

Ointment of Iodoform.

℞   Iodoformi ....   ℥ j
     Cosmolinæ...............................   ℥ j
  Reduce the iodoform to powder and add to the vaseline; heat by water-bath till dissolved.

Ointment of Peruvian Balsam.

R Bals. Peru.................................... ℥ ij
Cerat. simplicis.............. .... ℥ j
M.

Dusting Powder.

Take of—
Camphor .... dr. 1
Talc..
Zinc oxide ....of each... dr. 6
M.

Compound Oil of Cade Ointment.

R Ol. cadini.................................... f℥ j
Ung. zinci oxidi......................... ℥ j

Compound Iodoform Ointment.

R Pulv. iodoform.........................
Acidi tannici......................āā... ℥ j
Cosmolinæ .... ℥ j

Ointment of Tar and Oxide of Zinc.

R Ung. picis................................. ℥ iv
Zinci oxidi............................... ℥ j
Cerat. simplicis.......................... ℥ jss

Lead and Zinc Ointment.

℞   Plumbi acetat ....   gr. x
     Zinci oxidi.................................
     Hydrarg. chlor. mitis..................
     Ung. hydrarg. nitratis............āā...   gr. xx
     Adipis recentis............ ....
     Olei palmæ purific...............āā...   ℥ ss

Ointment of Mercury and Iodine.

℞   Ung. hydrarg ....
     Ung. iodin. comp..................āā...   ℥ j

Tannic Acid Ointment. (*Stronger.*)

℞   Acidi tannici.............................   ℥ j
     Ung. simplicis...........................   ℥ j

Eczema Drying Salve.

℞   Plumbi glycerat........................   ℥ j
     Ung. zinci oxidi ....   ℥ j

—o—

MIXTURES.

Emulsion of Cod-liver Oil with Solution of Saccharated Lime.

(75 per cent. emulsion.)

℞   Ol. morrhuæ...............................   ℥ vj
     Ol. anisi.....................................   ℥ ss
     Ol. sassafras........ ....   gtt. x
     Liquor. calc. sacchar...................   ℥ ij
   M.
Not compatible with acids.

Chlorate of Potassium Mixture.

℞ Ammon. muriat...........................
Potass. chlorat...................āā... ℨ j
Ext. glycyr................................. ℨ ss
Aquæ cinnam.....................ad... ℥ iv
   M.—Dose, a tablespoonful.

———

Mixture of Iodide of Potassium and Hoffman's Anodyne.

℞ Potass. iodidi............................. ℨ iij
Spt. ether. comp......................... ℨ j
Syr. pruni virg............................ ℨ iij
   M.—Dose, a teaspoonful.

———

Ether Cough Mixture.

℞ Ether. sulph.............................. ℨ iij
Tinct. hyoscyam.........................
Syr. pruni virg............................
Syr. tolutan......................āā... ℨ j
Aquæ.............................ad... ℥ iv
   M.—Dose, two to four drachms.

———

Chloroform Cough Mixture.

℞ Morphiæ acet............................. gr. iij
Tr. belladonæ............................. ℨ iv
Spt. chloroformi......................... ℨ vj
Syr. senegæ............................... ℨ j
Syr. pruni virg.................ad... ℥ iv
   M.

Hydrocyanic Mixture.

℞ Potassii cyanidi.......................... gr. ij
   Syrupi tolut...............................
   Liq. morph. sulph., U. S.P.....āā... ℥ j
   M.—Dose, a teaspoonful.

Ward Cough Mixture.

℞ Fld. ext. pruni virg..................... ℥ iij
   Sol. potassii cyanidi.................... gr. viij
   Sol. morphiæ Magendie............... ℥ ss
   Glycerinæ.................................. ℥ x
   Aquæ....................................... ℥ xviij
   M.—Dose, a teaspoonful p. r. n.

Mixture of Sulphate of Magnesia and Iron.
(*A.*)

℞ Magnes. sulph............................ ℥ j
   Ferri sulph............................... gr. xvj
   Acidi sulph. dil......................... f. ℥ ij
   Syr. zingib............................... f. ℥ j
   Aquæ....................................... ℥ vij
   M.

(*B.*)

℞ Magnes. sulph............................ ℥ j
   Ferri sulph............................... ℥ j
   Acidi sulph. aromat..................... ℥ ij
   Tinct. gentian........................... ℥ j
   Aquæ....................................... ℥ iij
   M.—Teaspoonful after eating.

(*C.*)

℞ Ferri sulph...............................   gr. xvj
    Magnes. sulph........ ....   ℥ j
    Acidi sulph. arom............ ....   f℥ ss
    Aq. menthæ pip...................ad...   O j
M.

Mixture of Iron and Cinchona.

℞ Ferri et ammon. citratis...............   ℥ j
    Tinct. nucis vom......................…....   ℥ ij
    Tinct. cinchon. comp..................   ℥ iv
M.—Dose, a teaspoonful.

Alkaline Mixture.

(*A.*)

M Potass. acetat......................…......   ℥ ij
    Potass. et sodii tartrat...…..............   ℥ j
    Syr. zingiberis...........…...............   f℥ j
    Aquæ...........................…............   ℥ iij
M.

(*B.*)

℞ Potass. citrat.........................…......   ℥ j ss
    Syr. limonis...........................
    Aquæ.............................āā...   ℥ iij
M.

Nitrous Acid Mixture.

℞ Tr. opii deod............................   f℥ ij
    Acidi nitrosi.......................…....   f℥ ss
    Aq. camphoræ ....…..ad...   f℥ iv
M.

Mixture of Mercury and Iodide of Potassium.

(*A.*)

℞   Hydrarg. bichlor......................... gr. j
    Potass. iodid............................. ℥ ij
    Tr. cardam. comp.......................
    Tr. gentian.....................āā... ℥ j
   M.—Dose, one drachm.

(*B.*)

℞   Hydrarg. bichlor......................... gr. j¼
    Potass. iodid............................. ℥ iij
    Tr. cardamom. comp................... ℥ ij
   M.—Dose, one drachm.

(*C.*)

℞   Hydrarg. biniod......................... gr. ss
    Potass. iodidi............................. ℥ j
    Syr. sarsap. comp....................... ℥ j
   M.—Dose, one drachm three times a day.

(*D.*)

℞ No. 1. { Hydrarg. bichloridi.............. gr. j
       Potass. iodid....................... ℥ iv
       Ferri et ammon. cit.............. ℥ j
       Aquæ.......................ad... ℥ j

℞ No. 2. { Tinct. nuci. vom.................. ℥ ij
       Tinct. cinchon. comp......ad... ℥ iij

Mix No. 1 and No. 2 at time of dispensing, and label "Shake Well."

Dose, ℥ j., t. i. d.

(℔.)

℞ Hydrarg. ᴅɪɴɪoᴅ....................... gr. j
Potass. iodidi........................... ℥ v
Syr. aurant. cort........................ f ℥ ij
Tr. card. comp.................. .... f ℥ ij
Aquæ.......................q. s...ad... i ℥ jv
M.

Arsenious Acid Tonic.

℞ Acidi arseniosi........................... gr. 1-5
Ferri et quin. cit........................ gr. lxxx
Tr. cinch. comp....................ad... f ℥ ij
M.

Compound Acid Tonic.

℞ Tr. nucis vomicæ..................... f ℥ ij
Acid. nitro-muriat. dil............... f ℥ iij
Tr. cinch. comp...................... f ℥ j ss
Tr. gent. comp..................ad... f ℥ iij
M.—Dose, two drachms in water, three times a day.

Hamilton's Tonic.

℞ Strychniæ sulph....................... gr. viij
Cinchonidiæ sulph..................... ℥ j
Tr. ferri chlor....................... ℥ vj
Tinct. zingib......................... ℥ ij
Glycerinæ................... .. ..
Acid. phosphoric. dil...........āā... ℥ xvj
M.—Dose, one teaspoonful three times a day.

Effervescing Mixture.
No. 1.

℞ Acidi citrici...................................
Ferri et quiniæ cit................āā...   ℥ iv
Aquæ.....................................
Syr. limonis.......................āā...   f℥ ij
M.

No. 2.

℞ Potass. bicarb............................   ℥ iv
Aquæ.................................ad...   ℳ iv

M.—One fluid drachm of each in two drachms of water, to be mixed at the time of taking.

Mixture of Rhubarb and Soda.

℞ Pulv. rhei.................................   gr. xlv
Sodii bicarb..............................   ℥ j ss
Aq. menth. pip....................ad...   f℥ ij
M.

Rochelle Salt Mixture.

℞ Sodii et potass. tart......................   gr. cmlx
Ferri et potass. tart......................   gr. cccxx
Aquæ menth. pip.........................   f℥ iv
Aquæ...............................ad...   O
M.

Mixture of Squill, Compound.

℞ Ammon. chlor............................   ℥ ij
Potass. chlorat...........................   ℥ j
Syr. scillæ comp.........................   f℥ ss
Syr. tolut.................................   f℥ vj
Liq. ammon. acet................ad...   f℥ iij

Mixture of Quinia, Compound.

℞   Quiniæ sulph...........................   ʒ ij
     Acid. sulph. ar........................   f ʒ iv
     Tinct. cinch. comp...........…ad...   f ʒ iij
   M.

Carminative Mixture.

℞   Tr. opii................................   gtt. xx
     Ol. anisi............... ....
     Ol. caryophyl...........................
     Ol. gaulth........................ .āā...   gtt. ij
     Tr. asafœtidæ...........................   f ʒ j
     Magnes. carbon........................   ʒ j
     Aquæ menthæ pip.................ad...   f ʒ iij
   M.

Anti-Rheumatic Mixture.
(Mistura Antiarthritica.)

℞   Potassii iodidi.........................   ʒ v
     Vini colchici sem.....................   ʒ j
     Tr. cimicifugæ rac...................   ʒ ij
     Tr. stramon............ ....   ʒ ss
     Tr. opii camph.......................   ʒ j ss
   M.—Dose, ʒ j, three times a day.

La Fayette Mixture.

℞   Bals. copai væ.........................
     Spt. ether. nit........................
     Spt. lavand. comp.................āā...   ʒ iv
     Liquor potassæ........................   ʒ iv
     Mucilag. acac....................ad...   O ij
   M.

Mixture of Digitalis Compound.

℞   Inf. digital..................................   ℥ j
    Potass. brom..............................   ℥ j
  M.

Compound Infusion of Buchu.

℞   Fol. buchu.................................   ℥ j
    Tritici repentis...........................   ℥ jss
    Potass. acet...............................   ℥ iij
    Acaciæ gran...............................   ℥ j
    Aquæ ferv................q. s...ad...   O ij
  M.—Ft. infusion.

Mixture of Bicyanide ef Mercury.

℞   Hydrarg. bicyanidi.....................   gr ss
    Potass. iodid.............................   ℥ ij
    Tr. cardam. comp.......................   ℥ ss
    Syr. sarsap. comp......................
    Aquæ........................ āā...ad...   ℥ ij
  M.

—o—

MISCELLANEOUS.

Syrup of Hypophosphites Compound.

℞   Calcii hypophos.........................
    Sodii hypophos...................āā...   gr. ij
    Potassii hypophos......................
    Ferri hypophos...................āā...   gr. j
    Acidi hypophos solut...........q. s...
    Glycerinæ...............................
    Aquæ...................āā...q. s...ad...   ℥ j
  M.

Bitter Wine of Iron.

R   Ferri et quiniæ cit......................   gr. lxiv
Tr. aurant. amar.......................   f℥ ij
Elix. simplicis......... ....   f℥ j
Vini Xerici.............................   f℥ ij
Aquæ.....................q. s....ad...   f℥ iv
M.

Errhine Powder.

R   Pulv. cubebæ...........................   ℥ ss
Sodii bicarb.............................   ℥ ij
Acidi salicylici...........................   gr. x
Sacch. alb ....   ℥ ij
M—Fiat pulvis.

Fasciculus Sennæ Comp.

R   Fol. sennæ...............................
Quassiæ.......................āā...   ℥ ij
Potass. bitart............................   ℥ j
Semin. anisi.............................   ℥ ss
M.

Suppositories of Ergot.

R   Ext. ergot. aquos. (Squibb's).........   ℈ ij
Ol. theobromæ..........................   ℥ j
M.—Div. in supposit. No. xij.

Solution of Acetate of Ammonium.

R   Liq. ammon. acet. conc...............   ℥ j
Aquæ acidi carbonici.................   ℥ xv
M.

Concentrated Solution of Acetate of Ammonium.

℞   Acid. acetic...........................   ℥ ij
    Aquæ fervent.................... ......   ℥ ij
    Ammonii carbonat....................   q. s.
Ft. sol. neutral.   Evaporate to ℥ ij.   This keeps well.

—— o ——

HYPODERMIC SOLUTIONS.

Carbolized Distilled Water.

℞   Acidi carbolici.........................   1 part
    Aquæ destillatæ.......................   999 parts

Ext. Ergot Solution.

℞   Ext. ergot (Squibb's)................   1 part
    Aquæ destil. carbol..................   5 parts

Magendie's Sol. Morphia.

℞   Morphiæ sulph........................   gr. lxxx
    Aquæ destil carbol...................   f. ℥ v
    M. and filter.

Hypodermic Solution of Quinine.

℞   Quiniæ sulph..........................   grs. clx
    Acid. hydrobrom, (Squibb's)........   f. ℨ j
    Spts. frumenti....................ad...   f. ℥ j
    M. ft. solut.

Sol. Pilocarpia Muriate.

R   Pilocarpiæ mur........................   gr. j
     Aquæ dest. carbol........................   m l

M.—Dose, ten minims.

Sol. Apomorphia Muriate.

R   Apomorphiæ muriat. cryst............   gr. j
     Aquæ dest.............................   m ixxx

M —Dose, m x, for emetic.
To be prepared only at the time it is wanted.

— o —

POWDERS.

The following powders are sent to the wards and dispensed in bulk, and measured out to the patient in a small measure equal to about 20 grains.

Pulvis S. I. C.

R   Sodii bicarb............................   600 parts
     Ipecac...................................   I part
     Cubebæ.................................   300 parts

M.—Dose, one measure.

Pulvis P. B. S.

R   Pepsinæ.......................................
     Bismuth....................................
     Sodii bicarb.....................āā...   100 parts

M.—Dose, one measure,

Pulvis B. I. C. S.

℞ Bismuth. subnit............................ 200   parts
Ipecac.. 3¼   "
Cubebœ...................................... 200   "
Sodii bicarb................................ 400   "
M.—Dose, one measure.

—o—

PILLS.

Triplex Pills.

℞ Hydrarg, mass...........................
Pulv. aloes........................āā...   gr. ij
Pulv. scammon. res....................   gr. j
M. ft. pil. No. j.

Laxative Pills.

℞ Podophyl. res............................   gr. ⅓
Ext. bellad...............................   gr. ¼
Ext. nuc. vom...........................   gr. ⅓
M. ft. pil No. j

Compound Podophyllin Pills.

℞ Res. podophylli..........................   gr. ½
Ext. nuc. vom...........................   gr. ⅓
Aloes purif...............................   gr. j
Ol. anisi..................................   gtt. 1-6
M. ft. pil. No. j.

Rhubarb and Soda Pills.

℞ Rhei pulv...............................
Sodii bicarb......................āā....   gr. jss
Ipecac......................................   gr. 1-10
M. ft. pil. No. j.

Carmalt's Piils.

R Res. podophylli........................ gr. ¼
Ext. nuc. vom...........................
Aloes purif.....................āā... gr. 1-6
Ext. hyoscyami......................... gr. ½
M. ft. pil. No. j.

Fothergill's Pills,

R Morph. mur........................... gr. 1-6
Atropiæ sulph........................... gr. 1 60
Pulv. capsici........................... gr. ½
Pil. aloes et myrrhæ................... gr. j ss
M. ft. pil. No. j.

Clark's Pills.

R Quiniæ sulph........................... gr. 3 ⅓
Pulv. capsici........................... gr. j
Pulv. opii........................... gr. ⅓
M. ft. pil No. j.

Pills of Lead and Opium.

R Plumbi acet........................... gr. ij
Pulv. opii..........................., gr. ¡
M. ft. pil. No. j.

Diuretic Pills.

R Pulv. scillæ........................ ....
Pulv. digitalis.........................
Massæ hydrarg...................āā... gr. j
M. ft. pil. No. j.

Blaud's Pills.

℞ Ferri sulph..............................
Potass. carb......................āā... gr. ij ss
M. ft. pil. No. j.

___

Pills of Aloes and Iron.

℞ Ferri sulph. exsic......................... ℨ ss
Pulv. aloes purif......:................. ℨ j
Pulv. aromat............................. ℨ j
Conf. rosæ................................. ℨ j
M. fiant pil. No. xl.

___

Antiperiodic Pills.

℞ Quin. sulph............................. ℨ j
Pulv. capsici............................. gr. xv
Pulv. zingib............................. gr. xxx
M. div. in pil. No. xxx.

___

Pills of Hydrarg. Colocynth, and Ipecac.

℞ Ext. colocynth comp.....................
Mass. hydrarg....................āā... gr. x
Pulv. ipecac............................. gr. ij
M. div. in pil. No. iv.

___

Pills of Nux Vomica, compound.

℞ Ext. nucis vomicæ..................... gr. xxiv
Pulv. rhei...............................
Pulv. aloes.................. ......āā... gr. xxxvj
Podophylli resinæ..................... gr. viij
M. ft. massa, div. in pil. No. xlviij.

Compound Mercury Pills.

℞ Mass. hydrarg.......................... grs. ij
    Ferri sulph. exsic...................... grs. j
  M. ft. pil. No. j.

———

Compound Lupulin Pills.

℞ Lupulinæ................................ grs. iv
    Ext. hyoscyami....................... grs. 1-15
    Pulv. acaciæ........................... q. s.
  M. ft. pil. No. j.

———

Compound Pills of Hyoscyamus.

℞ Ext. hyoscyami...................... gr. ½
    Hydrarg. proto-iod.................. gr. ¼
    Ferri et quin. cit..................... gr. j
  M. et ft. pil. No. j.

———

Compound Iodoform Pills.

℞ Iodoformi............. .... gr. j
    Hydrarg. chlorid. corros.............. gr. 1-20
    Ferri redacti...... .... gr. j
  M. ft. pil. No. j.

———

Compound Chinoidine Pills.

℞ Chinoidinæ.............................
    Iodoformi..............................
    Ferri redacti.....................āā... gr. j
  M. ft. pil. No. j.

ROOSEVELT
HOSPITAL FORMULARY
(NEW YORK CITY.)

---o---

TONICS.

Cod-Liver Oil Emulsion.

℞   Cod-liver oil............................... ℥ ij
    Glycerine................................... ℥ j
    Gum arabic, powdered................. ℥ j
    Water, s. q................................. ℥ ss

M.—Dose, ℥ ss

Cod-Liver Oil with Hypophosphites.

℞   Hypophos. lime......................... gr. x
    Hypophos. soda......................... gr. v
    Hypophos. potass....................... gr. v
    Hypophos. iron.......................... gr. v
    Dil. phosphoric acid, s. q............
    Cod-liver oil.............................. ℥ ij
    Glycerine .... ℥ j
    Boiling water s. q....................... ℥ ss

M.—Dose, ℥ ss.

Arsenical Mixture.

℞ Sol. potass. arsenite........................ ♏ ij
    Comp. infus. gentian.................... ℥ ss
    Water, s. q.............................. ℥ j
    M.—Dose, ℥ j.

Iron and Arsenic.

℞ Sol. chlorid. arsen........ ⎫
    Tinct. chlorid. iron...... ⎬ of each,   ♏ ij
    Water, s. q............................ ℥ j
    M.—Dose, ℥ j.

Compound Cod-Liver Oil.

℞ Cod-liver oil .... ℥ ss
    Syr. lactophosph. lime................. ♏ xv
    Syr. iodide iron....................... ♏ iv
    Sol. lime, s. q........................ ℥ j
    M.—Dose, ℥ j.

Laxative Iron Mixture.

℞ Sulph. magnesia........................ ℥ ss
    Sulph. iron............................ grs. ij
    Dil. sulph. acid................s. q...
    Comp. tinct. gentian................... ♏ xv
    Water, s. q............................ ℥ ss
    M.—Dose, ℥ ss.

Child's Tonic.

℞   Ammon. cit. iron........................   grs. v.
        Sol. arsenite potass....................   ℥ ij
        Syr. orange.............................   ℥ ss
        Water, s. q..............................   ℥ j

M.—Dose, ℥ j for a child three years old.

Quinine, Iron and Arsenic.

℞   Sol. arsenit. potass....................   ℥ iij
        Cit. iron and quinine...................   gr. v
        Comp. tinct. gentian s.q..............   ℥ ij

M.—Dose, ℥ ij

Bright's Tonic.

℞   Sulph. strychnine ....   gr. 1-32
        Tinct. chlor. iron......................   ℥ xv
        Simple syrup...........................   ℥ j
        Water, s. q.............................   ℥ ij

M.—Dose, ℥ ij

Effervescing Iron.

℞   Cit. iron and quin......................   grs. 5⅝
        Citric acid...............................   grs. 7½
        Water, s. q..............................   ℥ ij

M.—Label, A. solution. Dose, ℥ ij; mix with ℥ ij of
B. solution.

℞   Bicarb potass............................   grs. 18¾
        Water, s. q..............................   ℥ ij

M —Label, B. solution. Dose, ℥ ij; mix with ℥ ij of
A. solution.

Tincture of Iron.

R Tinct. chlor. iron.......................... ♏ xv
    Glycerine.................................... ℥ ss
    Cinnamon water, s. q................... ℥ ij
    M.—Dose, ℥ ij.

———o———

COUGH MIXTURES.

Mixture No. 1.

R Sulph. morphine........................ gr. 1-16
    Chloride ammon......................... gr. 2½
    Syrup tolu................................ ♏ xv
    Water, s. q. to........................... ℥ ij
    M.—Dose, ℥ ij.

Mixture No. 2.

R Fl. ex. wild cherry bark............... ♏ 5⅜
    Sol. cyanid. potass. ⎰ 16 grs. ⎱ āā... ♏ 15-16
    Sol. sulph. morph. ⎱ to oz. ⎰
    Simple syrup, s. q. to.................. ℥ ij
    M.—Dose, ℥ ij.

Codeine Mixture.

R Codeine.................................... gr. 1-6
    Dil. phosphoric acid.................... ♏ v
    Simple syrup, s. q. to.................. ℥ j
    M.—Dose, ℥ j.

Ipecac Mixture.

℞   Wine of ipecac...... .... ♏ v
    Muriat. of ammon...................... gr. v
    Camphor water, s. q. to.............. ℥ ss

M.—Dose, ℨ ss.

Antimony Mixture.

℞   Tartrat. antim and potass.............. gr. 1-24
    Sulph. morph........................... gr. 1-10
    Syr. wild cherry bark, s. q........... ℨ i

M.—Dose, ℨ j.

Sanguinaria Mixture.

℞   Tinct. sanguinaria...................... ♏ v
    Carbon. ammon....................... grs. v
    Syr. wild cherry bark, s. q........... ℨ j

M.—Dose, ℨ j.

Carbon. and Iodide Ammon. Mixture.

℞   Carbon. ammon....................... grs. iij
    Iodide ammonium..................... grs. ij
    Simple syrup........................... ℨ j

M.—Dose, ℨ j.

Atropine Mixture.

℞   Sulph. atropine........................ gr 1-128
    Sulph. quinine......................... grs. ix
    Dil. sulph. acid, s. q..................
    Simp. syrup, s. q. to.................. ℥ i

M.—Dose, ℨ j in water.

Children's Mixture.

R Paregoric.................................... ♏ x
   Muriate ammon......................... grs. v
   Syrup squills............................. ♏ x
   Syrup tolu, s. q. to..................... ℥ j
   M.—Dose, ℥ j.

Hydrobromic Mixture.

R Dil. hydrobromic acid (10 per ct.)..
   Spirits chloroform......... of each.... ♏ iv
   Syrup squills............................. ♏ viij
   Paregoric, s. q. to....................... ℥ ij

Bromide and Hyoscyamus Mixture.

R Bromide potass.......................... grs. xx
   Tinct. hyoscyam....................... ℥ ss
   Camphor mixt., s. q. to.............. ℥ ss
   M.—Dose, ℥ ss.

Squills Mixture.

R Tinct. squills............................. ♏ v
   Wine of ipecac.......................... ♏ iv
   Syrup of tolu............................ ♏ xx
   Water, s. q............................... ℥ j
   M.—Dose, ℥ j for child one year old.

Chloride of Ammon. Mixture.

R Chloride ammon........................ grs. ij
   Syrup wild cherry bark............... ℥ ss
   Water, s. q. to.......................... ℥ j
   M.—Dose, ℥ j for child one year old.

Emphysema Mixture.

℞   Iodid. potass......................................   gr. v
     Tinct. belladon..............................   ℳ v
     Comp. spir. ether..........................   ℳ xlv
     Magend. sol. morph.....................   ℳ ij ss
     Water, s. q...................................   ℥ ss
     M.—Dose, ℥ ss.

——o——

DIARRHŒA MIXTURES.

Nitric Acid.

℞   Nitric acid...................................   ℳ xx
     Tinct. opium...............................   ℳ vij ss
     Tinct. camphor..........................   ℳ vij ss
     Comp. syr. rhubarb....................   ℥ j
     Syr. ginger................................   ℥ j
     Water, s. q...............................   ℥ j
     M.—Dose, ℥ j.

Kino and Opium (Dysentery.)

℞   Tinct. kino................................   ℳ xx
     Tinct. catechu..........................   ℳ xx
     Tinct. opium.............................   ℳ xv
     Tinct. capsicum......................   ℳ v
     M.—Dose, ℨ j (in water.)

Bismuth and Soda.

℞   Sub. nit. bismuth.......................   grs. iij
     Bicarb. soda.............................   grs. ij
     Peppermint water.....................   ℨ ss
     Chalk mixture, s. q....................   ℨ ij
     M.—Dose, ℨ ij.

Opium and acid.

℞ Comp. sol. opium, Squibb's.......... ♏ x
Arom. sulph. acid...................... ♏ x
Water, s. q.
M.—Dose, ℥ ij.

Compound Bismuth.

℞ Camph. tinct. opium............. ...... ♏ x
Subnit. bismuth...................... grs. x
Chalk mixture, s q.................... ℥ ij
M.—Dose, ℥ ij as directed. Shake.

Compound Chalk.

℞ Camph. tinct. opium.................. ♏ v
Tinct. krameria....................... ♏ v
Comp. spirits lavend.................. ♏ ij
Chalk mixture, s. q................... ℥ j
M.—Dose, ℥ j, as directed.

Aromatic Rhubarb.

℞ Powd. bicarb. soda.................... grs. ij
Aromatic syr. rhubarb................. ♏ xx
Syrup ipecac............. .... gtt. v
Glycerine............................. ℥ ss
Cinnamon water, s. q................. ℥ j
M.—Dose, ℥ j.

Chalk and Catechu.

℞ Tinct. opium.......................... ♏ vij ss
Chalk mixture......................... ℥ j
Tinct. catechu, s. q.................. ℥ ij
M.—Dose, ℥ ij, as directed. Shake.

Coto.

℞ Fl. ex. coto bark...................... ♏ ij
    Glycerine................................. ℥ ss
    Water, s. q.............................. ℥ j
    M.—Dose, ℥ j.

West.

℞ Castor oil................................. ℥ j
    Powd. acacia........................... grs. xx
    Sugar.;.................................... ℥ ss
    Tinct. opium............................ ♏ iv
    Spirits nutmeg.......................... ♏ xx
    Orange flower water.................. ℥ xj
    M.—Dose, ℥ j.

MIXTURES FOR DYSPEPSIA, ETC.

R. & S. Compound.

℞ Tinct. nux vomica..................... ♏ v
    Powd. ipecac........................... gr. ¼
    Bicarb. soda............................ grs. v
    Powd. rhubarb......................... grs. ij
    Peppermint water,................... ℥ j
    M.—Dose, ℥ j.

R. & S.

℞ Powd. rhubarb......................... grs. ij
    ‘   bicarb. soda..................... grs. v
    “   ipecac............................ gr. ¼
    Peppermint water, s. q............... ℥ ij
    M.—Dose, ℥ ij.

Pepsine.

℞ Saccharat. pepsine...................... grs. iij
Dil. muriat acid....................... ℳ iij
Glycerine................................. ℳ v
Water, s. q............................... ℥ j
M.—Dose, ℥ j.

Dyspepsia Mixture.

℞ Dil. hydrochloric acid.................. ℳ x
Tinct. nux vomica...................... ℳ x
Tinct. cinchona, s. q.................. ℥ j
M.—Dose, ℥ j.

Colic Mixture.

℞ Spirit of chloroform................... ℳ xx
Arom. spirit of ammon................ ℳ xx
Comp. spirit lavend.................. ℳ xx
M.—Dose, ℥ j.

Infant Laxative Mixture.

℞ Nitrate potass.......................... gr. j
Sulph. magnes.......................... grs. v
Lemon syrup............................ ℥ ss
Water, s. q.............................. ℥ j
M.—Dose, ℥ j for a child one year old.

Rhubarb and Magnesia Mixture.

℞ Sulph. magnes.......................... grs. v
Tinct. rhubarb.......................... ℳ iij
Syr. ginger............................. ℳ x
Peppermint water, s. q............... ℥ j
M.—Dose, ℥ j for a child one year old.

Castor Oil.

℞   Castor oil.................................. ℥ j
     Glycerine .... ℥ ss
     Ol. cinnamon............................. ♏ ⅛

M.—Dose, ℥ jss.

Vinum Gastricum.

Take one perfectly fresh calf's rennet, cut up into pieces and put in a jar, and pour on one quart of good sherry; do not filter. Dispense supernatant fluid after standing thirty-six hours.

——o——

SEDATIVES.

Chloral.

℞   Chloral hydrate......................... grs. vij ss
     Bromide potass.. .... grs. vij ss
     Orange flower water................... ♏ xv
     Water, s. q............................ ℥ j

M.—Dose, ℥ j.

Jim Jam.

℞   Bromide potass......................... grs. xxx.
     Hydrat. chloral........................ grs. xv
     Magend. sol morph .... ♏ v
     Syr. orange peel....................... ℥ j
     Water, s. q............................ ℥ iv

M.—Dose, ℥ ss, as directed.

222222

Mixed Bromide.

℞ Bromide sodium........................ grs. x
Bromide potass........................ grs. xx
Bromide ammon........................ grs. x
Syr. orange peel..................... ℨ ij
Water, s. q........................... ℨ iv
M.—Dose, ℨ iv.

Bromide Solution.

℞ Bromide sodium .... grs. xv
Water................................ ℨ j
M.—Dose, ℨ j.

Hysteria.

℞ Tinct. castor........................ ♏ vj
Comp. tinct. valerian, s. q........... ℨ j
Dil. phosphoric acid.................. ♏ vj
M.—Dose, ℨ j.

Sound Mixture.

℞ Tr. aconite root..................... ♏ v
Sulph. morph......................... gr. 3-16
Water, s. q.......................... ℨ ij
M.—Dose, ℨ ij, as directed.

Elixir of Guarana.

℞ Fl. ex. guarana...................... ♏ x
Simple elixir, s. q.................. ℨ ?

DIURETICS.

Buchu Mixture.

R   Fl. ex. buchu.............................   ℥ ss
      Tinct. hyoscyam........................   ℥ ss
      Sol. citrat. potass.......................   ℥ j
    M.—Dose, ℥ ij.

Digitalis.

R   Infus. digitalis............................   ℥ j
      Acet. potass..............................   grs. xv
      Water, s. q................... ....   ℥ ij
    M.—Dose, ℥ ij.

—o—

ANTI-SYPHILITIC MIXTURES.

Mixed Treatment.

R   Bichlorid mercury......................   gr. 1-32
      Iodide potassium.......................   grs. x
      Comp. syr. sarsap......................   ℥ ss
      Water, s. q..............................   ℥ ij
    M.—Dose, ℥ ij.

Iodide Potassium.

R   Iodide potassium........................   grs. x
      Comp syr. sarsap......................   ℳ xv
      Water, s q...............................   ℥ j
    M.—Dose, ℥ j.

Saturated Sol. Iodide Potassium.
I—I
℥ j sol. represents ℥ j iodid. potass.

MISCELLANEOUS.

Iodide and Colchicum.

℞ Iodide potassium........................ grs. x
Wine colchicum seed.................. ℳ xx
Comp. syrup sarsap................... ʒ j
Water, s. q............. .... ℥ ss
M.—Dose, ℥ ss.

Sol. Salicylate Soda.

℞ Salicylate soda............ .... grs. x
Bicarb. soda, s. q......................
Powd. ext. licorice.................... grs. iij
Glycerine...... .... ℳ xl
Water, s. q............................ ʒ ij
M.—Dose, ʒ ij.

Infant Febrifuge.

℞ Citrat. potass......................... grs. iij
Bicarb. potass......................... grs. ij
Syr. lemon.............................. ʒ ss
Water, s. q............................ ʒ j
M.—Dose, ʒ j for child 1 year old.

Lafayette Mixture.

℞ Copaiba ....
Spt. nitrous ether......................
Comp. spt. lavender.............āā... ʒ ss
Sol. potassa........................... ℳ vij ss
Mucilage, s. q......................... ℥ ss
M.—Dose, ʒ ss.

R. H. Formula for Sol. Morph. Magend. for Hypodermic Use.

℞ Sulph. morphine........................ grs. xvj
    Salicylic acid........................... gr. ½
    Distilled water, s. q.................... ℥ j

Dissolve the salts in the water previously heated to the boiling point.   Filter.

Saturated Sol. Chlorat. Potass.

1—16.

Sol. Ergot for Hypodermic Use.

℞ Ext. ergot, Squibb's...................... ℥ ij
    Glycerine................................. ℥ ss
    Water..................................... ℥ j ss
    M.

Ward Solut. Atropine.

℞ Sulph. atropine.......................... gr. 1-96
    Water .... ℥ j
    M.—Dose, ℥ j.

Chloroform and Whisky.

℞ Chloroform............................... ♏ x
    Whisky, s. q............................. ℥ ss
    M.—Dose, ℥ ss.

PILLS.

Compound Arsenic Pills.

R Arsenious acid................... ....   gr. 1-20
   Reduced iron...........................   gr. j
   Sulph. quinine...........................   grs. ij
   M.—Make one pill.

Aloe and Iron.

R Dried sulph. iron.......................   gr. j
   Socot. aloes.............................   grs. j ss
   Arom. powd., s. q......................
   M.—Make one pill.

R. S. and I. Pill.

R Powd. rhubarb...........................   gr. j
   Bicarb. soda...........................   gr. j
   Ipecac................................. ....   gr. ⅛
   M.—Make one pill.

Iodoform.

R Iodoform........... ....   1 gr
   Make one pill.

Compound Diuretic.

R Corrosive sublim.......................   gr. 1-32
   Powd. squills ....   gr. j
   Powd. digitalis.......................   gr. j
   M.—Make one pill.

Hyoscyamus and Oxide Zinc.   Sweat Pill.

R   Ext. hyoscyamus.... ....   gr. ij
      Oxide zinc.................................   gr. iij
      Honey, s. q...............................
      M.—Make one pill.

Quinine (1 grain).

R   Sulph. quinine........................   gr. j
      Honey, s. q...............................
      M.—Make one pill.

Quinine (3 grains.)

R   Sulph. quin................... ....   grs. iij
      Honey, s. q...............................
      M.—Make one pill.

Blaud's.

R   Sulph. iron...............................   grs. ij ss
      Carb. potass.............................   grs. ij ss
      Pulv. tragacanth, s. q..................
      M.—Make one pill.

Laxative.

R   Ext. nux vom.................. ....   gr. ¼
      Ex. belladon...........................   gr. 1–6
      Comp. ex. colocynth..................   grs. ij
      Powd. socot. aloes....................   gr. j
      M.—Make one pill.

Codeine.

℞ Codeine .... gr. ½
Glycerole of starch, s. q..............
M.—Make one pill.

———o———

CAPSULES.

Quinine.................................... grs. 10
Quinine .... grs. 5
Salicylic................................... grs. 10
Salicylic................................... gra. 5

POWDERS

Bismuth, Pepsine, and Morphine.

10 grs.   10 grs.   1–6 gr.

Santonine

℞ Santonine............................... grs. ij
Sugar milk............................... grs. ij
M.—Make one powder.

Infant Calomel.

℞ Calomel................................. gr. j
Sugar..................................... grs. iij
M.—Make one powder.

Clark's Powder.

R   Sulph. quin..............................   grs. x
     Powd. capsicum........................   grs. v
     Powd. opium............................   gr. j
M.—Make one powder.

—o—

POWDERS IN BULK.

Dose, one measure represents about twenty grains.

Caiomel and Jalap Comp.

R   Calomel...................................   grs. x
     Comp. powd. jalap.....................   grs. x
M.

Soda.

R   Bicarb. soda...........................   grs. z⁻

Bismuth and Soda.

R   Subcarbon. bismuth...................   grs. x
     Bicarb. soda...........................   grs. x
M.

Ipecac and Soda.

R   Pulv. ipecac............................   gr ¼
     Bicarb. soda............................   grs. xx
M.

Bismuth, Cubeb, and Soda.

R Subnit. bismuth......................... ⎫
Pulv. cubeb............................. ⎬ equal parts.
Pulv. bicarb. soda..................... ⎭
M.

Bismuth and Pepsine.

R Subnit. bismuth.......................... grs. x
Pepsine .... grs. x
. M.

Alkaline Laxative.

R Chloride sodium.......................... ℥ j
Bicarb. soda............................... ℥ iv
Carbon calcium........................... ℥ j ss
Sulph. soda................................. ℥ j ss
M.—Dose, ℥ ij.

——o——

EXTERNAL APPLICATIONS.

——— .

Evaporating Lotion.

R Muriat. ammon......................... ℥ ss
Alcohol...................................... ℥ iv
Water, s. q................................. O j
M.—External use.

Red Wash.

R Sulph. zinc................................. grs. xvj
Comp. spirit lavend..................... ℥ ss
Water, s. q................................... O j
M.

Churchill's Tinct. Iodine.

R   Iodine.................................   grs. lxxv
      Iodide potassium.......................   grs. xv
      Alcohol ....   ℥ vj
      Water.................................   ℥ ij

M.—For external use.

Sol. Carbolic Acid and Glycerine.

R   Carbolic acid, pure.....................   ℥ j
      Glycerine, pure.......................   ℥ j

M.—C. A. and G. As a base for dispensing for internal use.

Comp. Tinct. Green Soap.

R   Green soap........................... ⎫
      Oil cade.............................. ⎬ equal parts.
      Alcohol.............................. ⎭

Dissolve the green soap in the oil of cade with the aid of heat. Add the alcohol and shake. For external use.

Sol. Lead and Opium.

R   Sol. subacet. lead......................   ℥ j
      Tinct. opium..........................   ℥ ss
      Water, s. q...........................   O j

M.—External use.

Alkaline Lotion.

R   Bicarb soda...........................   grs. x
      Biborat soda......... ....   grs. x
      Cherry laurel water....................   ℥ j

M.

Sulphurous Acid Lotion.

℞ Sulphurous acid........................ ℥ j
   Water..................................... ℥ iij

M.—External use.

Comp. Chloroform Liniment.

℞ Chlorof. commercial...............⎫
   Tinct. opium.........................⎬ of each ℥ j
   Tinct. camph........................⎭
   Tinct. capsic............................. ℥ ss

M —External use.

Liniment Stimulant.

℞ Ammonia water......................... ℥ ss
   Tinct. capsicum........................ ℥ ss
   Soap liniment........................... ℥ j

M.—External use.

Borated Solution.

℞ Salicylic acid............................ 1 part.
   Boric acid................................. 6 parts.
   Water...................................... 500 "

M.

Chloroform and Aconite Liniment.

℞ Commercial chloroform............... ℥ j
   Tinct. aconite root..................... ℥ j
   Soap liniment .... ℥ ij

M.—External use.

Ward Gargle.

℞ Biborate soda............................ ℨ j
   Sat. sol. chlorate potass............... ℨ j
   Water, s. q............................. ℥ viij

M.—Use as a gargle.

Chloride Zinc Gargle.

℞ Chloride zinc........................... grs. x
   Glycerine............................... ℥ ss
   Water, s. q............................. ℥ iv

M.—Use as a gargle.

Tannin and Alum Gargle.

℞ Alum...... .... ℨ ss
   Tannin.................................. ℨ ss
   Glycerine............................... ℥ ss
   Water, s. q .... ℥ iv

M.—Use as a gargle.

Alkaline Tar Water.

℞ Liquid tar.............................. ℥ ij
   Caustic potass......................... ℨ j
   Water............................ .... ℥ v

M.—External use.

OINTMENTS.

Salicylic and Zinc Ointment.

℞ Salicylic acid.......................... grs. xv
   Powd. oxide zinc....................... ℨ ij ss
   Powd. starch........................... ℨ ij ss
   Petroleum............ .... ℥ j

M.

Carbolic Ointment, 3 per ct.

R   Carbolic acid........................ ....   gr. I
Petrolatum................. ....   grs. 33⅓

Cade and Zinc.

R   Oil of cade.............................   ℨ j
Oxide of zinc ointment...............   ℨ j
M.

Iodoform.

R   Iodoform........... ....   ℨ j
Petrolatum............................   ℨ j
M.

Balsam Peru Ointment (Strong Brown Ointment.

R   Salicylic acid............................   I part
Bals. Peru..............................   5 parts
Petrolatum..............................   II "
M.

Balsam Peru Ointment (Mild).

R   Bals. Peru oint. strong.................   I part
Petrolatum......................................   6 parts
M.

Boric Acid.

R   Boric acid..............................   I part
Petrolatum............ ....   6 parts
M.

Tube Iodoform Ointment.

℞   Expressed oil almonds................   9 parts
      Spermaceti.............................   1 part
      Wax.....................................   1 "

Melt together at a moderate heat the oil of spermaceti and wax, stirring the mixture constantly until it is nearly cool, then add powdered iodoform in the proportion of one part of iodoform to four of the ointment, and continue the stirring until it has become uniformly soft.

Chrysarobin Gelatine.

Dissolve one part pure gelatine in two parts water in water-bath, and add ten per cent. chrysarobin.

Pyrogallol Gelatine.

10—20 per cent.

Salicylated Gelatine.

5—10 per cent.

Dusting Powder.

℞   Camphor...................................   ℨ j
      Talc....................... ....   ℨ vj
      Oxide zinc............. ....   ℨ vj
    M.

Public Charities and Correction,

BELLEVUE HOSPITAL.

Hydrocyanic Mixture.

℞   Potass. cyanidi..........................
Morphiæ sulphat..................āā...   grs. 4
Syr. tolut...............................   fl. ℥ 4

M.—Each ℨ contains ⅛ grs. each of potassium cyanide and morphia sulphate.   Dose, a teaspoonful.

Rhubarb and Soda.

℞   Sodii bicarbon...........................   ℨ 1
Pulv. rhei...............................   ℨ ½
Spt. menthæ pip.....................   fl. ℨ 2
Aquæ,....................q. s...ad...   fl. ℥ 4

M.—Dose, a tablespoonful.

Tincture of Phosphorus.

℞ Phosphori...................................... grs. 32
    Alcoholis absol............................ fl. ℥ 46
    Tr. vanillæ.................................. fl. ℥ 1
    Ol. aurantii cort.......................... fl. ℥ 3
    Alcoholis absol............q. s...ad... fl. ℥ 48

The phosphorus is digested with the absolute alcohol, with the exclusion of air, until dissolved; then the flavoring ingredients are added, and finally the bulk is made up with absolute alcohol to 48 fl. oz.

12 fl. drachms contain 1 grain of phosphorus.

30 minims contain 1–24 grain of phosphorus.

Dose, 20-40 minims, corresponding to 1–36—1–18 gr. of phosphorus.

Anti-Rheumatic Mixture.

℞ Sodii et potass. tart...................... ℥ ½
    Potass. nitrat............................. ℥ 5
    Vin. colchici sem........................ fl. ℥ 2
    Aquæ....................q. s...ad... fl. ℥ 2

M.—Dose, a teaspoonful.

Thomson's Tonic.

℞ Ferri et ammon. cit...................... ℥ 1
    Ammon. carbonat....................... gr. 30   •
    Tr. gentian comp......................
    Tr. quassiæ.......................āā... fl. ℥ 2
    Syrupi...................................... fl. ℥ 1 ½
    Aquæ ....q. s...ad... fl. ℥ 8

M.—Dose, a tablespoonful.

Dr. W. H. Thomson.

Phosphorated Cod-Liver Oil.

℞   Olei phpsphorati* (1 per cent)......   grs. **100**
     Ætheris.................................   fl. ℥   **2**
     Olei morrhuæ...........q. s...ad...   fl. ℥   16

M.—Two hundred and thirty-three minims, or practically ½ fl. ℥, contain 1–30 grain of phosphorus. The phosphorated oil should be weighed, not measured.

———o———

OUT-DOOR DEPARTMENT, BELLEVUE HOSPITAL.

Whooping-Cough Mixture.

℞   Tinct. nucis vom........................   fl. ℥ 2
     Vin. ipecac.............................   fl. ℥ 2½
     Syr. sarsap. comp.......................
       " senegæ.......................āā...   fl. ℥ 1½
M.—Dose, a teaspoonful, for children.

Dr. Ackermann.

---

*Oleum Phosphoratum.

℞   Phosphori..............................   gr. **1**
     Olei morrhuæ..........................   grs. 99

This is a 1 per cent. solution of phosphorus in cod-liver oil, proposed by Dr. E. R. Squibb. It is made with the utmost care, and contains the full amount of phosphorus. If only a portion of the contents is to be used, a few drops of ether should be poured into the vial, before it is again corked and sealed. If a fine film should form on the surface or at the bottom, the oil must be poured out, so as to leave this in the vial. Should this film increase, or much of a precipitate make its appearance, a fresh bottle should be used.

It is best to add the whole contents of a bottle at once to sufficient cod-liver oil to be ready for administration. The latter may be kept on hand in full and well-closed bottles, which are to be kept in the dark.

When using the phosphorated oil it should always be taken by *weight.*

Cough Mixture.

℞   Syr. tolut..
    Syr. pruni. virg............................
    Tr. hyoscyami............................
    Spt. ætheris comp.....................
    Aquæ..............................āā... fl. ℥ 1
    M.—Sig   Dose, a teaspoonful.

Prof. E. G. Janeway.

Expectorant Mixture for Children.

℞   Syr. senegæ.............................
    "   pruni virg...........................
    "   accaciæ......................āā... fl. ℥ 1
    M.—Dose, a teaspoonful

Dr. Holgate.

Mistura " Bronchi."

℞   Ammonii carbon......................... grs. 10
    Syr. ipecac............................. fl. ℥ 1½
    Tr. opii camph......................... fl. ℥ 1
    Syr. pruni virg........................
    Aquæ....................q. s...ad... fl. ℥ 2
    M.—Dose. a teaspoonful for children.

Dr. Beverly Robinson.

Carbonate of Ammonia Mixture.

℞   Ammonii carbonat..................... ℥ ½
    Syr. senegæ............................ fl. ℥ 4
    "   ipecac............................... fl. ℥ 2
    "   tolut................................. fl. ℥ 4
    Ext. glycyrrhizæ....................... ℥ ½
    Aquæ cinnam.............q. s...ad... fl. ℥ 4
    M.—Dose, a teaspoonful, for children.

Dr. Geo. H Bosley

Chloride of Ammonium Mixture.

R Ammonii chloridi............................ ℥ ½
Potassii chlorat............................ grs. 40
Syr. senegæ .... fl. ℥ 4
" ipecac .... fl. ℥ 3
" tolut.................................... fl. ℥ 5
Ext. glycyrrhizæ .... ℥ 1
Aquæ cinnam..............q. s...ad... fl. ℥ 4

M.—Dose, a teaspoonful, for children.

Dr. *Geo S. Bosley.*

Expectorant Mixture.

R Syr. scillæ comp........................
Syr. ipecac.....................āā... fl. ℥ 1
Syrupi .... fl. ℥ 1

M.—Dose, a teaspoonful, for children.

Dr. *Swezey.*

Licorice Mixture.

R Ammonii chloridi........................
Ext. glycyrrhizæ.................āā... ℥ 2
Tr. opii camph.......................... fl. ℥ 2
Aquæ....................q. s...ad... fl. ℥ 4

M.—Dose, a teaspoonful.

Dr. *Brekes.*

Sedative Mixture.

R Acid. hydrocyan. dilut.................
Chloroformi purif.................āā... fl. ℥ 1
Tr. hyoscyami............................
Syr. tolutani............................
Aquæ camphoræ.................āā... fl. ℥ 1

M.—Dose, a teaspoonful.

Dr. *Katzenbach.*

Hoffmann's Anodyne and Iodide of Potash.

R Potass. iodidi............................ ℥ 3
   Tr. tolut.....................................
   Ext. pruni virg. fl...............āā... fl. ℥ 1
   Syrupi....................................... fl. ℥ 1
   Spt. ætheris comp...................... fl. ℥ 2
   Aquæ .... fl. ℥ 1
  M.—Dose, a teaspoonful.

Prof. E. G. Janeway.

Nitrate of Potash Mixture.

R Potass. nitrat............................ gr. 1
   Spt. æther nit...........................
   Syr. ipecac....................āā... fl. ℥ ½
   Syr. pruni virg........................... fl ℥ 2
   Aquæ....................q. s...ad... fl. ℥ 1
  M.—Dose, a teaspoonful, for children

Chlorate of Potash Mixture.

R Potass. chlorat........................... ℥ 1
   Ext. glycyrrhizæ........................ ℥ ½
   Ammonii chloridi....................... ℥ 1
   Aquæ....................................... fl. ℥ 4
  M.—Dose, a teaspoonful.

Dr. Geo. G. Wheelock

Hoffman's Anodyne and Iodide of Potash.

R Ammonii carb........................... grs. 50
   Potass. iodidi........ .... ℥ 3
   Syr. pruni virg..........................
   Spt. æther. comp................āā... fl. ℥ 1½
  M.—Dose, a teaspoonful.

Dr. Katzenbach.

Cyanide and Bromide of Potash Mixture.

℞   Potass. bromidi..............................   ℥ 4
     Potass. cyanidi............................   grs. 4
     Syr. pruni virg............................ fl ℥ 4
     M.—Dose, a teaspoonful

Opium, Rhubarb and Camphor.

℞   Tr. opii ....
     Tr. rhei arom.............................
     Spt. camphoræ....................āā... fl. ℥ ½
     Tr. cardam. comp .... fl. ℥ 2
     Aquæ anisi...................q. s...ad... fl. ℥ 4
     M.—Dose, a tablespoonful, for children in diarrhœa.
                         Dr. Swezey.

Castor Oil Mixture.

℞   Olei ricini............................... fl. ℥ 4
     Mucil. acaciæ...........................   ℥ 4
     Tr. opii .... fl. ℥ 2
     Tr rhei. arom. .... fl. ℥ 4
     Aquæ menthæ pip........q. s...ad..... fl. ℥ 4
     M.—Dose, a teaspoonful, for children, in diarrhœa.
                         Dr. Bosley.

Rhubarb and Soda.

℞   Sodii bicarb..............................   ℥ 1
     Ext. rhei. fl............................. .....
     Spt. menthæ pip.................āā... fl. ℥ 1
     Aquæ......................q. s...ad... fl. ℥ 4
     M.—Dose, a tablespoonful.

Bicarbonate of Soda.

℞ Sodii bicarb............................... ℥ 1
   Tr. zingiber .... fl. ℥ 2
   Tr. gent. comp .... fl. ℥ 1
   Aquæ .... fl. ℥ 5

M.—Dose, two teaspoonfuls.

Rhubarb and Lime.

℞ Tr. opii camph ....
   Syr. rhei. arom....................āā... fl. ℥ ½
   Aquæ calcis........................ ..... fl. ℥ 2

M.—Dose, a teaspoonful, for children, in diarrhœa.

Dr. Ackermann.

Pulv. Bismuthi, Cretæ et Opii.

℥ Bismuth. sub-nit...................,..... grs. 30
   Cretæ præcipit........................... grs. 30
   Pulv. opii................................. gr. 1

M.—Divide into 10 powders. For children in diarrhœa.

Dr. J. Lewis Smith.

Pulv. Bismuthi et Doveri.

℞ Bismuthi sub-nit......................... grs. 4
   Pulv. ipecac comp...................... gr. 1

M.—One dose for children, in diarrhœa.

Pulv. Bismuthi et Pepsini.

℞ Bismuthi sub-nitr......................
   Pepsini............................āā... gr. 3

M.—One dose, for children.

Dr. Swezey.

Pulvis Bismuthi Comp.

℞ Bismuthi sub-nit.........................
Sodii bicarb..............................
Pulv. sacchari...........................
Pulv. acaciæ............................
Pulv. zingiber....................āā...   p. e.

M.—Dose, a tablespoonful, for adults, in dyspepsia.
Dr. Wheelock.

Salicylic Acid Mixture.

℞ Acidi salicylici...........................   grs. 160
Potass. acetat...........................   grs. 320
Glycerinæ................................   fl. ℥ 1
Aquæ.......................q. s...ad...   fl. ℥ 4

M.—Dose, a teaspoonful.

Syrup of Biniodide of Mercury.

℞ Potassii iodidi..........................   grs. 80
Hydrarg. biniodidi....................   gr. 1½
Syrupi..   fl. ℥ 2

Dissolve and mix. Dose, a teaspoonful.
Dr. Banks.

Thompson's Mixed Treatment.

℞ Hydrarg. biniodidi....................   gr. 1
Potassii iodidi...........................   ℈ 3
Tr. aurantii...............................   fl. ℥ 1
Aquæ.......................................   fl. ℥ 3

M.—Dose, a teaspoonful.
Dr. Beverhout Thompson.

Taylor's Mixed Treatment.

℞ Hydrarg. biniodidi......................   gr. 1
    Potass. iodidi...........................   Ʒ 4
    Syr. sarsap. comp.......................
    Aquæ..........................āā... fl. Ʒ 2

    M.   *Dr. R. W. Taylor.*

Muriatic Acid Mixture.

℞ Acidi muriatici........................ fl. Ʒ 3
    Tr. gent. comp.........................
    Aquæ.......................āā... fl. Ʒ 8

    M.—Dose, a teaspoonful.

Pil. Ferri Quin. et Strych.

℞ Quiniæ sulph........................:....
    Ferri redacti.....................āā...   Ʒ 1
    Strychniæ acetat......................   gr. 1
    Ext. gentian..........................   q. s.

    M.—Divide into sixty pills.

Iron and Citrate of Ammonia.

℞ Ferri et ammon. cit................... .
    Ammonnii carbon...... ....āā...   grs. 32
    Syrupi...................................
    Aquæ anisi....................āā... fl. Ʒ 2

    M.—Dose, a teaspoonful.

                  Dr. J. L. Smith.

Iron and Cinchona.

℞ Cinchonæ sulph ....   Ʒ 1
    Tr. ferri chloridi..................... fl. Ʒ 2
    Aquæ ....q. s. ad... fl. Ʒ 4

    M.—Dose, a teaspoonful.

Lemon Tonic.

℞ Cinchonæ sulph........................... grs. 30
   Acidi sulph. dil........................... q. s
   Aquæ.. fl. ℥ 1
   Acidi citrici.................... ..... ℥ ½
   Syrupi............................ .... fl. ℥ 1½
   Tr. ferri chlor .... fl. ℥ ½
   Aquæ .. ..q. s. ad... fl. ℥ 4
   M.—Dose, a teaspoonful.

Sulphate of Cinchona.

℞ Cinchonæ sulph................. .... ℥ 1
   Acidi sulphur. dil....................... q. s.
   Aquæ..................................... fl. ℥ 4
   M.—Dose, a teaspoonful.

Iodide Mixture.

℞ Potassii iodidi   .... ℥ 4
   Syr. ferri iodidi......................... fl. ℥ 1
   Tr. calumbæ............. q. s. ad... fl. ℥ 4
   M.—Dose, a teaspoonful.

——o——

External Applications—

Ung. Hydr. Ox. Rub. c. Plumbo.

℞ Hydrarg. oxidi rubri................... .
   Plumbi acetat....................āā... grs.
   Cerati.............. .... ℥ 1
   M.

Dr. McKay.

Sulphur Paste.

℞ Sulphuris sublimati.....................   ℥ 1
    Ætheris........................... fl. ℥ 3
    Glycerinæ............... .... fl. ℥ 1
M.

———

Ung. Picis Alkalinum.

℞ Liquoris picis alkalini................. fl. ℥ 1
    Cerati........................... ....   ℥ 1
M.

———

Dr. R. W. Taylor's Lotion.

℞ Sulphuris sublimati.....................   ℥ 3
    Spt. camphoræ.......................... fl. ℥ 2
    Sodii biboratis...........................   ℥ 1
    Glycerinæ .... fl. ℥ 3
    Aquæ........... ....   ℥ 6
M.

———

Carson's Paint.

℞ Olei tiglii................................ fl. ℥ ½
    Ætheris...... .... fl. ℥ 1
    Tr. iodinii comp........................ fl. ℥ 2½
M.—Counter irritant and vesicant in pleurisy, etc.

Emulsion—
Cod Liver Oil Mixture.

℞ Olei morrhuæ............................ fl ℥ 16
Liquor potassæ.......................... fl ℥ 2
Mellis....................................... fl. ℥ 3
Pulv. acaciæ............................. ℥ 1
Ol. anisi.................................. gtt. 20
Ol. menthæ vir.......................... gtt. 18
M.—Dose, a tablespoonful.

Dr. Winston.

—o—

CHARITY HOSPITAL, BLACKWELL'S ISLAND.

Expectorant Mixture.

℞ Tr. sanguinar............................ fl. ℥ 1
Tr. opii camph..........................
Syr. scillæ................................
Syr. tolut......................āā ... fl. ℥ 2
Aquæ ....q. s. ad... fl. ℥ 2
M.—Dose, a teaspoonful.

Asthmatic Mixture.

℞ Spt. æther comp........................
Liquor morph. sulph. (U. S.)....āā... fl. ℥ 1
M.—Dose, from one teaspoonful to a tablespoonful.

Hydrocyanic Mixture.

℞ Potass. cyanidi............................ grs. 2
   Vini antimonii........................... fl. ℥ 2
   Syr. tolut...............................
   Mucil. acaci....................āā... fl. ℥ ½
   Aquæ ....q. s. ad... fl. ℥ 1
   M.—Dose, one teaspoonful.

Hot Drops.

℞ Tr. opii...................................
   Tr. capsici...............................
   Spt. camphoræ...........................
   Spt. menthæ pip.................āā... fl. ℥ 2
   Aquæ............................. fl. ℥ 1
   M.—Dose, a teaspoonful.

Anti·Emetic Mixture.

℞ Creasoti................................. ℳ 12
   Acid. hydrocyan. dil..................... ℳ 30
   Pulv. acaciæ.........-..................
   "   sacchari ....āā... ℥ 6
   Aquæ......................q. s. ad... fl. ℥ 2
   M —Dose, a teaspoonful.

Anti-Rheumatic Mixture.

℞ Sodii et potass. tart..................... ℥ ½
   Vini colchici sem....................... fl, ℥ 2
   Aquæ.......................q. s. ad... fl. ℥ 2
   M.—Dose, a teaspoonful.

Iodide of Potash Mixture.

℞   Potass. iodid.............................   ℥ 4
      Syr. sarsap. comp........................
      Tr. gent. comp...............āā... fl. ℥ 1
  M.—Dose, a teaspoonful.

Lemon Tonic.

℞   Cinchonæ sulph......................... grs. 30
      Acidi sulph. dil........................... q.s.
      Aquæ.. fl. ℥ 1
      Acidi citrici............................... ℥ ½
      Syrupi....................................... fl. ℥ 1 ½
      Tr. ferri chlor .... fl. ℥ ½
      Aquæ........................ ad... fl. ℥ 4
  M.—Dose, a teaspoonful.

Cod-Liver Oil Mixture.

℞   Olei morrhuæ...........................
      Aquæ calcis.....................āā... fl. ℥ 8
      Olei cinnamomi......................... gtt. 10
  M.—Dose, a tablespoonful.

Solution Ergotine.

℞   Ergotini................................... gr. 36
      Glycerinæ.................................
      Aquæ..........................āā... ♏ 108
  M.

INSANE ASYLUM, BLACKWELL'S ISLAND.

Expectorant Mixture.

℞   Spt. etheris comp ....
     Syr. ipecac...............................
     Tr. opii camph ....
     Aquæ...............................āā...   p. e.

M.—Dose, a teaspoonful.

Cannabis Mixture.

℞   Tr. cannabis Ind ....   ♏ 10
     Spt. menthæ pip.........................   ♏ 1
     Aquæ ....q. s. ad... fl. ʒ 1

M.—One dose.   To be taken thrice daily after meals.

Epileptic Belladonna Mixture.

℞   Potass. bromidi....................... grs. 25
     Tr. belladonnæ .... ♏ 5
     Aquæ ....q. s. ad... fl. ʒ 1

M.—One dose to be taken thrice daily.

Sedative Mixture.

℞   Chloralis ....:................ grs. 15
     Extr. conii sem. fl................. .....
     Extr. hyoscyam fl.............āā... ♏ 16
     Aquæ ....q. s. ad... fl. ʒ 1

M.—One dose, to be taken thrice daily, after meals.

Epileptic (Conium) Mixture.

℞   Potass. bromidi............................ ℥ ½
    Ext. conii fl............................... ♏ 15
    Aquæ ....q. s. ad... fl. ℥ 1

M.—One dose, to be taken thrice daily.

Epileptic (Ergot) Mixture.

℞   Potass. bromidi..... ....
    Ammon bromidi...................āā... ℥ ½
    Ext. ergotæ fl............................ ♏ 15

M.—One dose; to be taken thrice daily, in cases characterized by considerable maniacal excitement following the attack, indication of cerebral congestion and especially where hemmorhage is feared.

Dr. Chas. R. Smith.

Strychnine Tonic.

℞   Tr. ferri chloral ....
    Tr. nucis vom .. ..āā... ♏ 10
    Aquæ.......................q. s. ad... fl. ℥ 1

M.—One dose, to be taken thrice daily, after meals.

NINETY-NINTH STREET RECEPTION HOSPITAL.

Pilulæ Aloes et Fellis.

℞   Ext. aloes................................. grs. 30
    Fellis bovis purif....................... grs. 20
    Resin. podophylli...................... grs. 2½

M.—Divide into ten pills.   Dose, one pill at night in chronic constipation; one pill night and morning in acute constipation.

Laxative Pills.

R Pulv. rhei..
Pulv. aloes........................āā... grs. 15
Ext. bellad ....
Ext. nucis vom ....
Resin. podophylli..............āā... grs. 3
Olei caryophylli....................... gtt. 5

M.—Divide into twelve pills. Dose, one pill mornings and evenings.

Anti-Epileptic Pill.

R Argenti nitrat........................ gr. 10
Zinci oxidi............................ gr. 20
Micæ panis........................... q. s

M.—Divide into twenty pills. Dose, one pill thrice daily.

Croton Oil Liniment.

R Olei tiglii................................ fl. ℥ 2
Olei olivæ ....
Olei terebinthinæ....................
Aquæ ammoniæ.....................
Spt. camphoræ .....āā p.e. q.s. ad... fl. ℥ 2

M.—S. Externally in chronic muscular pains.

HART'S ISLAND HOSPITAL.

Anti-Rheumatic Mixture.

R Potass. iodid........................... ℥ 1
"   acetat... .... ℥ 4
Tr. colchic' sem...................... fl. ℥ 2
Aquæ....................................... O 2

M.—Dose, a tablespoonful.

Expectorant Emulsion.

℞ Morph. sulph................................ grs. 2
    Syr. scillæ..................................
      " ipecac.......................āā... fl. $\bar{3}$ 2
      " tolut...........................
      " pruni virg..................āā... fl. $\bar{3}$ 1½
    Tr. benz.......................
    Tr. sanguinariæ...................āā... fl. $\bar{3}$ ½
    Aquæ...... .... fl. $\bar{3}$ 2
    M.—Dose, a teaspoonful.

Diarrhœa Mixture.

℞ Tinct. capsici.............................. fl. $\bar{3}$ 1
      " catechu...........................
      " kino..............................
      " krameriæ ....āā... fl. $\bar{3}$ 4
      " opii.............................. fl. $\bar{3}$ 3
    Spt. menth. pip......................... fl. $\bar{3}$ 2
      " camphoræ...........................
    Aquæ..........................āā... fl. $\bar{3}$ 4
    M.—Dose, 30–60 minims.

INFANT'S HOSPITAL, RANDALL'S ISLAND.

Whooping-Cough Mixture

℞ Acid. nitric. dil............................ fl. $\bar{3}$ 1
    Syr. pruni virg......................... fl. $\bar{3}$ ½
    Aquæ...... ....q. s. ad... fl. $\bar{3}$ 2
    M.—Dose, a teaspoonful.

Pulv. Bismuthi et Pepsini.

℞ Bismuthi sub-carb.......................
Pepsini.......................... āa... grs. 2
M.—One dose for children.

Diarrhœa Mixture.

℞ Bismuthi sub-carb...................... grs. 2
Acid tannici............................... gr. 1
Pulv. ipecac comp...................... gr. ¼
M.—One dose for children in diarrhœa.

Cough Mixture for Infants.

℞ Tr. opii camph..........................
Spt. ammon. arom...............āā... fl. ℥ 1
Ext. ipecac fl............................. fl. ℥ ½
Syr. pruni virg.......................... fl. ℥ 1
Aquæ ....q. s. ad... fl. ℥ 3
M.—Dose, a teaspoonful

FORMULARY

OF THE

Long Island College Hospital,

(BROOKLYN, N. Y.)

MIXTURES.

1.—Mixture of Citrate of Iron and Quinine.

R   Ferri et quiniæ cit........................   ℥ ss
      Syr. simplicis.............................   ℥ ij
      Aquæ.....................................   ℥ v
  M.

2.—Mixture of Pyrophosphate of Iron.

R   Ferri pyrophos...........................   ℥ ss
      Tr. gentianæ comp....................   ℥ iij
      Aquæ.....................................   ℥ v
  M.

3.—Mixture of Iron and Cinchona.

℞ Cinchoniæ sulphatis....................... ʒ j
    Tr. ferri chloridi........................ ʒ iv
    Tr. quassiæ............................... ʒ j
    Aquæ....................q. s...ad... ʒ iv
  M.

4.—Mixture of Sulphate of Quinia.

℞ Quiniæ sulphatis........................ grs. x
    Acidi sulph. dil..................... .... q. s.
    Glycerinæ................................ ʒ ij
    Aquæ.............................ad... ʒ j
  M.

5.—Mixture of Acetate of Iron.

℞ Tr. ferri chloridi....................... ʒ ij ss
    Spt. vini rect........................... ʒ j
    Acidi acetici............................ ʒ ss
    Liq. ammon. acetat...................
    Syr. simplicis.........................
    Aquæ........................āā... ʒ j
  M.

6.—Mixture of Rhubarb and Soda.

℞ Ext. rhei fl............................... ♏ xl
    Ext. ipecac. fl........................... ♏ iij
    Sodii bicarbonatis..................... grs xl
    Aq. menthæ pip..........q. s...ad... ʒ ij
  M.

7.—Hydrocyanic Cough Mixture.

℞   Morphiæ sulphatis......................   gr. ij
     Acidi hydrocyanici dil................   ʒ ss
     Syr. scillæ...............................
     Syr. tolutanis..............āā...   ʒ ij
  M.

8.—Bromide Cough Mixture (Read).

℞   Potass. bromidi........... ....   ʒ ij
     Spt. ammon. arom......................   ʒ ij
     Syr. scillæ ....   ʒ j
     Aquæ.....................q. s...ad...   ʒ iij

Belladonna Cough Mixture.

℞   Ammon. chloridi.......................   ʒ ij
     Morphiæ sulphatis......................   grs. ij
     Tr. aconiti rad...........................   ♏ xvj
     Ext. belladonnæ fl.....................   ♏ v
     Ext. glycyrrhizæ fl.....................
     Syr. simplicis.................āā.....   ʒ j
     Aquæ.....................q. s...ad...   ʒ iv
  M.

10.—Compound Squills Cough Mixture.

℞   Syr. scillæ......................... ....
     Syr. acaciæ...... ....
     Spt. ætheris nitrosi.....................
     Tr. opii camph.................āā...   ʒ j
  M.

11.—Gastric Catarrh Mixture.

℞ Ammonii chloridi......................... grs. xl.
   Vini ipecacuanhæ...................... ℥ ss
   Acidi hydrochlor. dil.................. ℥ j
   Spt. rhei aromat........................ ℥ iv
   Syr. simplicis................q. s. ad... ℥ j
   M.

———

12.—Mixture of Mercury and Iodide of Potassium.

℞ Hydrarg. bichloridi..................... gr. ij
   Potass. iodidi............................. ℥ ss
   Potass. chloratis.......................... ℥ j
   Tr. gentianæ comp....................
   Aquæ......................āā... ℥ iv
   M.

———

13.—Mixture of Donovan's Solution and Iodide of Potassium.

℞ Hydrarg bichloridi..................... grs. ij
   Potass. iodidi............................. ℥ j
   Liq. arsen. et hydrarg. iod............ ℥ vj
   Tr. cinch. comp.......................
   Glycerinæ......................āā... ℥ iv
   Aquæ....................................... ℥ viij
   M.

14.—Lafayette Mixture.

℞ Balsamum copaibæ.......................
Spt. ætheris nitrosi..............āā... ℥ j
Liq, potassæ.............................. ℥ ij
Ext. glycyrrhizæ fl.................... ℥ iv
Olei gaultheriæ.......................... ℳ xvj
Syr. acaciæ............................... ℥ vj
M.

___

15.—Lafayette Mixture (Modified.)

℞ Balsamum copaibæ.............. .... ℥ j
Liq. potassæ.............................. ℥ ij
Syr. acaciæ............................... ℥ jss
Aq. menthæ pip.......... q. s...ad... ℥ iij
M.

___

16.—Clark's Mixture.

℞ Acidi salicylici........................... ℥ iij
Sodii bicarbonatis....................... ℥ ij
Glycerinæ................................
Aquæ ....aa... ℥ ij
M.

___

17.—Bismuth and Pepsin Mixture.

℞ Bismuth subnitratis..................... ℥ jss
Vini pepsinæ............................
Glycerinæ.........................āā... ℥ ss
Mist. cretæ ....q. s...ad... ℥ ij
M.

EMULSIONS.

18.—Emulsion of Cod-Liver Oil and Hypo phosphites.

℞ Olei morrhuæ...........................
    Syr. hypophos. comp............āā.....   ℥ iij
    Olei gaultheriæ...... ....   q. s.
    Mucilage acaciæ........................   ℥ ij
  M.

19.—Emulsion of Cod-Liver Oil and Gentian.

℞ Olei...............................
    Tr. gentianæ............................
    Syr. acaciæ comp..............āā...   ℥ ij
    Ol. gaulth.....................q. s....
  M.

PILLS.

20.—Arsenious Acid Pill.

℞ Acidi arseniosi...........................   gr. j
    Cinchonidiæ sulph......................   grs. xxx
    Pulv. capsici.............................   grs. iv
    Ext. cinchonæ...........................
    Pulv. chinoidini..............,......āā...   grs. xxx
  M. et ft. pil. No. xxx.

21.—Aloes and Belladonna Pill (R.)

℞   Ext. aloes aq.............................   grs. x

Cinchoniæ sulph........................   grs. xl

Ferri sulph. exsic......................   grs. xx

Ext. belladonnæ........................

Ext. nucis vomicæ............... āā...   gr. v

M. et ft. pil. No. xx.

——

22.—Aloes and Hyoscyamus Pill (R. H.)

℞   Pulv. aloes soc...........................

Quiniæ sulphatis.......................

Ferri sulphatis exsic..............āā...   grs. xx

Ext. nucis vomicæ.....................   grs. iv

Ext. hyoscyami........................   grs. xv

M. et ft. pil. No xx.

——

23.—Strychnia and Podophyllum Pill.

℞   Strychniæ sulphatis....................   gr. j

Resinæ podophylli....................   grs. x

Ext. colocynth. comp.................   grs. xl

Pulv. capsici...........................   grs. xx

M. et ft. pil. No. xl.

—o—

POWDERS.

24.—Bismuth and Soda.

℞   Bismuthi subcab...................... . grs. x

Sodii bicarbonatis.......................   grs. iij

M. et ft. chart. No. j.

25.—Calomel and Chalk (A.)

R Hydrarg. chlor. mite................... gr.
   Cretæ præparatæ........................ grs. viij
  M. et ft. chart. No. viij.

26.—Rhubarb and Ipecac.

R Pulv. ipecacuanhæ..................... grs.
   Pulv. rhei.............................. grs. xij
   Sodii bicarbonatis......................
   Pulv. cubebæ ....āā... grs. xxiv
  M. et ft. chart. No. vj.

27.—Magnesia and Potassium.

R Magnesii sulphatis.................... ℥ ij
   Potassii bitartratis.................... ℥ j
  M. et ft. chart. No. j

28.—Santonin (C. V. C.)

R Pulv. santonini......................... grs. x
   Hydrarg. chlor. mite.................. grs. iij
   Resinæ jalapæ.......................... gr. j
   Sacch. lactis............................ grs. xx
  M. et. ft chart. No. vj.

29.—Magnesia and Sulphur.

R Magnesii.............................
   Magnesii sulphatis....................
   Sulphuris..............................
   Sacch. albæ.......................āā... ℥ iv
   Pulv. anis.............................. ℥ ij
  M. et. ft. chart. No. j.

30.

R Sodii biboratis (in white paper)...... ℨ j

31.

R Potassii chloratis (in white paper)... ℨ ss

32.

R Zinci sulphatis (in blue paper)........ ℨ ss

——o——

FOR EXTERNAL USE.

33.—Aconite Liniment.

R Ext. aconiti rad. fl.....................
   Chloroformi.....................āā... ℨ j
   Spt. camphoræ......................... ℨ ss
   Lin. saponis ....q. s...ad... ℨ ij
  M.

34.—Rheumatic Liniment.

R Tr. capsici................................
   Aq. ammoniæ..........................
   Ol. terebinthinæ.......................
   Ol. olivæ.....................āā... ℨ j
   Tr. opii................................
   Tr. origani.................āā... ℨ ij
  M.

35.—Red Wash.

℞ Zinci sulphatis............................ grs. ij
   Tr. lavandulæ comp...................... ℥ xv
   Aquæ.. ℥ j
   M.

36.—Carbolized Wash.

℞ Acidi carbolici............................
   Glycerinæ.............................āā... ℥ j
   Aquæ.. O j
   M.

37.—Evaporating Lotion (Concentrated.)

℞ Ammon. chloridi......................... ℥ j ss
   Acidi acetici.............................. ℥ ij ss
   Spt. vini rectificati ....q. s...ad... ℥ iij
   M.—Sig. Dilute with one quart of water.

38.—Carbolized Oil.

℞ Acidi carbolici............................ ℥ j
   Olei olivæ.................................. ℥ ij
   M.

39.

℞ Atropiæ sulph............................ grs. ij
   Aquæ.. ℥ j
   M. et ft solutio.

40.

℞ Atropiæ sulph............................ grs. iv
   Aquæ .... ℥ j
   M. et ft. solutio.

OINTMENTS.

41.—Carbolic Acid Ointment.

R Acidi carbolici...........................
Glycerinæ............................āā...   ℥ j
Cerati simplicis..........................   ℥ j
M. et ft. unguentum.

42.—Carbolized Zinc Ointment.

R Acidi carbolici...........................   ℥ j
Unguenti zinci oxidi....................   ℥ j
M. et ft. unguentum.

43.—Tannic Acid Ointment.

R Acidi tannici..............................   ℥ ss
Adipis..................... ....   ℥ j
M. et ft. unguentum.

44.—Boracic Acid Ointment.

R Glycerit. acid. boracic. sat ....   ℥ ij
Ceræ albæ...............................
Cetacei.............. ....āā...   ℥ j
Ung. petrolei ....   ℥ vj
M. et ft. unguentum.

45.—Ointment of Iodoform and Balsam of Peru.

R Iodiformi .... ℥ j
  Bals. Peruviani............................. ℥ ij
  Ung. petrolei ⁚................................
  Adipis............................ ....
  Glycerinæ............................āā... ℥ j
  M. et ft. unguentum.

46.—Chrysophanic Acid Ointment.

R Acidi chrysophanici..................... ℥ ij
  Unguenti petrolei....................... ℥ xvj
  M. et ft unguentum.

47.—Calomel Ointment.

R Hydrarg. chlor. mite.................... ℥ ij ss
  Ung. aquæ rosæ .... ℥ xvj
  Ol. amygdal dulc........................... q. s
  M. et ft. unguentum.

48.—Ammoniated Mercury Ointment.

R Hydrarg. ammoniati.................... ℥ vj
  Ungt. petrolei .... ℥ xvj
  M. et ft. unguentum.

49.—Yellow Oxide of Mercury Ointment.

R Hydrarg. oxidi flav..................... grs. xvj
  Ung. petrolei........................----..... ℥ j
  M. et ft. unguentum.

50.—Diachylon Ointment—Hebra.

R︎ Olei olivarum.................. .... ℈ j
    Lithargyri..................... .... ℥ iij ss
Coque et add.
    Olei lavandulæ......................... ℨ ij
  M. et ft. unguentum.

Dr. Harrigan's Cough Mixture.

(Used in St. Mary's Hospital, Brooklyn, N. Y.)

R︎ Codeiæ.................................... gr. ¼
    Acidi hydrocyanici dil................. ♏ iij
    Syrup. prun. virg................. .... ℨ j
  M.– Sig. Above dose as required.

MEDICAL FORMULARY

OF THE

CITY ✸ HOSPITAL

OF THE

CITY OF BOSTON.

SOLUTIONS.

A.

			Grammes.
℞	Zinci sulphatis.....................	gr. iv	.26
	Aquæ...............	ℨ j	30.00

M.— ℨ j = gr. ss.

A. Dilut.

℞	Zinci sulphatis.....................	gr. ij	.13
	Aquæ..............	ℨ j	30.00

M.

A.—1.—3.

℞ Zinci sulphatis....................   gr. j| .065
   Aquæ...................... ....   ℥ j| 30.000
M.

A.—1.—7.

℞ Zinci sulphatis...................   gr. ss⌈   .032
   Aquæ...............................   ℥ j⌊   30.000
M.

Pilocarpina.

℞ Pilocarpinæ hydrochloratis.....   gr. ij | .13
   Aquæ...................... ....   ℥ j | 30.00
M.

Atropina.

℞ Atropinæ sulphatis...............   gr. ij| .15
   Aquæ...............................   ℥ j | 30.00
. M.

B.

℞ Sodii boratis.......................   gr. x | .65
   Aquæ camphoræ.................   ℥ j ⌋   30.00
M.

C.

℞ Potassii chloratis..................   gr. xv⌈   .97
   Aquæ...............................   ℥ j | 30.00
M.

D.

℞	Quininæ sulphatis...............	gr. viij	.52
	Acidi sulph. dil....................	ɱ viij	.52
	Aquæ.............................	℥ j	30.00

M.— ʒ j = *gr.* j.

F.

℞	Ferri sulphatis.....................	gr. iv	.26
	Magnesiæ "	gr. ix	3.88
	Acidi sulph. dil....................	ɱ xx	1.30
	Aquæ.............................	℥ j	30.00

M.

O.

℞	Tr. ferri chloridi.................	ɱ lxxx	5.00
	Aquæ........................ad...	℥ j	30.00

M.— ʒ j = ɱ x.

P.

℞	Potass iodidi.....................	gr. xl	2.50
	Aquæ........................ad...	℥ j	30.00

M.— ʒ j = grs. v.

P. B.

℞	Potass. bromidi..................	gr. lxxx	5.00
	Aquæ........................ad...	℥ j	30.00

M.— ʒ j = grs. x.

D. C.

℞ Hydrarg. chlor. corrosivi....   gr. ij | .13
    Tr. ferri chloridi...................   ℨ j | 30.00

M.—♏ x = gr. 1–34.

Chloral.

℞ Chloral..............................   gr. lxxx | 5.00
    Syrupi...............................   ℨ ss | 15.00
    Aquæ.........................ad...   ℨ j | 30.00

M.—ℨ j = grs. x.

Sodii Salicylas.

℞ Acidi salicylici.....................
    Sodii bicarb................āā...   gr. lxv | 4.21
    Syrupi...................... ....   ℨ ss | 15.00
    Aquæ.......................ad...   ℨ j | 30.00

M.

Ferri et Quininæ Citras.

℞ Ferri et quin. cit..................   gr. xl | 2.50
    Vini Xerici.................ad...   ℨ | 30.00

M.—ℨ j = gr. ꝟ.

MIXTURES.

I.

			Grammes.
℞ Sodii bicarb........................			
Rad. gentian. contus......āā...	℥	ss	15.0
Pulv. rhei.........................	ʒ	ij	7.5
" ipecac......................	ʒ	j	3.8
Aquæ bullientis.................	O	ij	960.0
M.—ft. infus.			

II.

℞ Hydrarg. chlor. corros.........	gr. ⅓		·02
Potass. iodidi....................	gr. xl		2.50
Syr. sarsæ comp............ad...	ʒ	j	30.00
M.			

III.

℞ Ferri sulphatis..................	gr. xxx		1.94
Syrupi............................			
Tr. quassiæ.................āā...	℥	ss	15.00
M.— ʒ j=grs. iij ss.			

IV.

℞ Hydrarg. biniodidi..............	gr. 2–5		.03
Potass. iodidi....................	gr. xl		2.59
Tr. iodi. æther..................	ℳ viij		0.52
Syr. ferri iodidi.................	ℳ cccxx		20.74
Aquæ.......................ad...	℥	j	30.00
M.			

V.

℞ Morphinæ sulphatis.............   gr. ½   .032
    Vini ipecac......................
    Syrupi senegæ...................
    " scillæ...................
    Aquæ ....āā...   ℥ ij   7 780
  M.

VI.

℞ Ammon. chlor..................   gr. lxxx   5.
    Ext. glycyrrhizæ fld............   ℥ iv   15.
    Spt. frumenti...................   ℥ iij   10.
    Syrupi.....................ad...   ℥ ij   60.
  M.

VII.

℞ Olei morrhuæ....................
    Spt. frumenti..............āā...   ℥ ss   15.00
  M.

VIII.

℞ Hydrarg chlor. corros...........   gr. ss   .032
    Potass. iodidi...................   gr. xl   2.500
    Tr. gentian. comp..............
    Aquæ.....................āā...   ℥ ss   15.000
  M.

IX.

℞ Liq. ammon. acet...............
    Spt. ætheris comp...............
    "   "   nit............āā...   ℥ j   30.00
  M.

X.

℞	Tr. camphoræ......................		
	Tr. opii............................		
	Tr. rhei.....................āā...	ʒ j	30.000
M.			

XI.

℞	Hydrarg. chlor. corros..........	gr. j	.064
	Tr. ferri chlor.....................	ʒ ss	15.000
	Aquæ..........................ad...	ʒ ij ss	77.000
M.			

XII.

℞	Vini antimonii....................	♏ x	.97
	Spt. ætheris nit..................	ʒ j	7.40
	Tr. opii deodor..................	♏ xxx	1·94
	Syrupi.....................ad...	ʒ j	30.
M.			

XIII.

℞	Morphinæ sulph..................	gr. ss	.032
	Chloroformi......................	♏ xx	1.30
	Glycerini........................		
	Aquæ.....................āā...	ʒ ss	15.00
M.			

XIV.

℞	Morphiæ sulph....................	gr. ss	.032
	Sodii "	gr. xxiv	1.560
	Aquæ............................	ʒ j	30.000
M.			

XV.

℞	Chloroformi	♏ xv	1.00
	Syr. pruni virg....		
	Syrupi.....................āā...	℥ ss	15.
M.			

XVI.

℞	Ammonii carb...................	gr. xvj	1.000
	" chlor.....................	gr. xl	2 500
	Morphiæ sulph...................	gr. ss	.03ᵥ
	Spt. anisi........................	ℨ ij	7.000
	Syr. p˙uni virg..............ad...	℥ j	30.000
M.			

XX.

℞	Olei lini sem....................		
	Syrupi.....................āā...	ℨ ss	15.000
	Olei amygdalæ amar...........	♏ v	.325
M.			

—o—

WASHES, ETC.

Carbolic Sol.

1—80.

℞	Acidi carbolici...................	℥ j	1.
	Aquæ ....ad...	O v	80.
M			

Carbolic Sol.
1—40.

℞ Acidi carbolici.....................   ℥ ij | 2.
   Aquæ..........................ad...   O v | 80.
M.

———

Carbolic Sol.
1—20.

℞ Acidi carbolici....................   ℥ iv | 4.
   Aquæ..........................ad...   O v | 80.
M.

———

Carbolic Oil.

℞ Acidi carbolici.....................   ℥ j | 4.
   Olei gossypii sem..........ad...   ℥ xx | 80.
M.

———

Chlorinated Soda Wash.

℞ Liq. sodæ chloratæ..............   ℥ j | 5.
   Aquæ..........................ad...   ℥ xvj | 80.
M.

———

Lead Wash.
("Liq. Plumb. subac. dil., U.S.P. 1880.)

℞ Liq. plumbi subacetatis.........   ℥ iij | 3.
   Aquæ..........................ad...   ℥ xij ss | 100.
M.

Myrrh Wash.

R Tr. myrrhæ....................... ℥ j | 1.
   Aquæ............................. ℥ iij | 3.
M.

Nitric Acid Wash.

R Acidi nitrici....................... ℥ j | 1.
   Aquæ.....................ad... ℥ xvj | 128.

Lead and Opium Wash.

R Tr. opii............................. ℥ ij | 1.
   Liq. plumbi subacet. dil........ ℥ xiv | 8.
M.

Soda and Opium Wash.

R Liq. sodæ chlor.................. ℥ ij | 2.
   Tr. opii............................... ℥ j | 1.
   Aquæ............................. ℥ x | 10.
M.

Chloroform and Aconite Liniment.

R Tr. aconiti rad..................... ℥ j | 30.
   Chloroformi.........   ....
   Lin. saponis................āā... ℥ ss | 15.
M.

Evaporating Lotion.

R Ammonii chlor.................... ℈ j | 1.
   Acidi acetici dil..................
   Spt. vini rect...................
   Aquæ.......................āā... ℥ iv | 32.
M.

Mouth Wash.

R Glycerini ....
  Aquæ rosæ..................āā...   ℥ ss | 15.
 M.

Alkaline Powders.

R Potassii bicarb......................
  Sodii..........................āā... gr. xv | .97
  Pulv. zingiberis.................. gr. ij | .13
 M.

—o—

OINTMENTS.

I.

Grammes.

R Ung. hydrarg. nit.................. ℥ j | 1.
  Ceratum........................... ℥ iij | 3.
 M.

II.

R Pulv. iodiformi.................. gr. xlviij | 10.
  Ung. petrolei.................... ℥ j | 90.
 M.

—o—

PILLS.

I.

R Hydrarg. iodid. vir.............. gr. ¼ | .016
  Ext. gentianæ.................... gr. ij | .130
 M.

II.

℞	Ferri sulph. exsic................	gr. j	.065
	Ext. nucis vom...................	gr. ¼	.016
	" aloes aq....................	gr. j	.065
M.			

III.

℞	Ferri sulph. exsic..............	gr. 3-5	.039
	Pulv. aloes......................		
	" capsici........ ......āā...	gr. j	.065
M.			

IV.

℞	Pulv. camphoræ................		
	" ipecac............		
	" opii ....āā...	gr. j	.065
M.			

V.

℞	Ext. colocynth. comp.........	gr. iij	.194
	" belladonnæ................	gr. 1-6	.010
M.			

VI.

℞	Ferri sulph. exsic................	gr. ij	.130
	Pulv. capsici......................		
	Ext. nucis vom...........āā...	gr. ss	.032
	Quininæ sulph................	gr. j	.065
M.			

VII.

℞	Pulv. opii...........................	gr. j	.065
	" cupri sulph................	gr. ¼	.016
M.			

VIII.

℞	Pulv. digitalis.....................	gr. j	.065
	" colchici sem................	gr. ss	.032
	" ipecac.......................	gr. 1-6	.010
M.			

IX.

℞	Ferri redacti.....................		
	Quininæ sulph............āā...	gr. j	.065
	Strychninæ sulph...............	gr. 1-60	.001
M·			

X.

(Pil. Ferri comp's., U.S.P., 1880.)

℞	Pulv. myrrhæ......	gr. j as	.097
	Sodii carb.........................		
	Ferri sulph................āā...	gr. ¾	.048
M.			

XI.

℞	Ext. hyoscyami................		
	Camphoræ................,.āā...	gr. ij	.130
M.			

XII.

℞ Pulv. digitalis...................... gr. ss ⎱ .032
    "   colchici.................... gr. j ⎟ .065
   Sodæ bicarb........................ gr. j ss ⎰ .097
M.

XIII.

℞ Res. podophyllin....... . . .... gr. ⅓ ⎱ .022
   Ext. colocynth. comp............ gr. iij ⎟ .195
   " byoscyami................. gr. j ⎰ .065

CHICAGO MARINE HOSPITAL.

U. S. MARINE–HOSPITAL SERVICE,

(*District of the Great Lakes.*)

———

PORT OF CHICAGO, ILL., SURGEONS'S OFFICE,
MAY 15, 1885.

DR. C. F. TAYLOR,
      Philadelphia.

Sir:—I have the honor to herewith transmit the formulæ in use at this hospital. Nos. 1 to 60 are kept constantly on hand, though the practice is not routine in the hospital here, and the ℞'s are prescribed where they meet the indications. They are not all original, and I would give credit if I knew to whom credit was due. I have no doubt you will find many of them duplicated from other sources. Where a "break" in numbers occurs it is by reason of retaining the hospital number, and well-known prescriptions like "Squibb's Mixture," "Brown-Sequard's Pills," etc., have been omitted. *I am not* responsible for the miserable Latin in some of the formulæ, as I could not write them myself.

        Yours truly,

            W. H. LONG, Surg. M. H. S.

(Note.—30 cubic centimeters equal ℥ 1.01. For

practical purposes, to reduce cubic centimeters to ounces, divide the number of cubic centimeters by thirty. One gram equals 15.432 grains, or about 15½ grains. To reduce grams to grains, multiply the number of grams by 15½.)

1.—Fever Mixture.

℞ Tr. aconit. rad.............................	20	c. c.
Spt. æther nit............................	200	"
Tr. cardam. comp.......................	150	"
Liq. ammon. acet................ad...	1000	"

M.—Dose, five cubic centimeters.

2.—Fever Mixture.

℞ Tr. aconit. rad...........................	30	c. c.
Tr. gelsemii............................	100	"
Tr. opii camph.........................	150	"
Pilocarpin mur........................	1	50 gm.
Liq. ammon. acet................ad...	1000	c. c.

M.—Dose, five c. c.

3.—Fever Mixture.

℞ Acid. hydrobrom. dil...................	300	c. c.
Tr. aconit. rad...........................	20	"
Quiniæ sulph.............	20	gm.
Spt. chloroformi........................	300	c. c.
Syr. simplicis..................ad...	1000	"

M.—Dose, five c. c.

4.—Rheumatic Mixture.

℞ Potass. iodid.............................. 150 | gm.
   Vin. colch. sem......................... 100 | c. c.
   Tr. cimicifugæ.......................... 300 | "
   Syr. sarsap. comp...................... 300 | "
   Aquæ.............................ad... 1000 | "

M.—Dose, five c. c.

5.—Rheumatic Mixture.

℞ Acid. salicylici........................ 50 | gm.
   Potass. bicarb......................... 100 | "
   Tr. aconit. rad........................ 5 | c. c.
   Ext. glycyrrhizæ fl.................... 50 | "
   Aquæ.............................ad... 1000 | "

M.—Dose, five c. c.

6.—Syphilitic Mixture.

℞ Hydrarg. chlorid. corros.............. 1 | gm.
   Potass. iodid.............. .... 100 | "
   Tr. gentian. comp..................... 300 | c. c.
   Extr. sarsap. comp. fl................. 100 | "
   Aquæ.............................ad... 1000 | "

M.—Dose, five c. c.

7.—Syphilitic Mixture.

℞ Potass. iodid........................... 150 | gm.
   Extr. stilling fl....................... 200 | c. c.
   Tr. cinchon. comp..................... 300 | "
   Aquæ.............................ad... 1000 | "

M.—Dose, five c. c.

8.—Cough Mixture.

R Ammon. chlorid........................ 100) gm.
Syr. senegæ..... .... 150 | c. c.
Syr. scillæ .... 150 | "
Syr. pruni virg.......:.................... 300 | "
Morphiæ chlorid........................ 1 | gm.
Extr. glycyrrhizæ fl.................... 100 | c. c.
Aquæ.........................ad... 1000 | "

M.—Dose, five c. c.

10.—Cough Mixture.

R Ammon. chlorid........................ 100) gm.
Potass. bromid........................... 100 | "
Tr. opii camph........................... 200 | c. c.
Syr. ipecac.............................. 200 | "
Syr. tolutan .... 300 | "
Ext. sarsap. comp. fl............ad... 1000 | "

M.—Dose, five c. c.

11.—Rheumatic Mixture.

R Potass. iodid........................... 100 | gm.
Ammon. chlorid........................ 100 | "
Tr. digitalis.............................. 100 | c. c.
Pilocarpin. chlorid...................... 2 | gm.
Mist. glycyrrhizæ..............ad... 1000 | c. c.

M.—Dose, five c. c.

13.—Diarrhœa Mixture.

R Tr. opii camph........................... 200) c. c.
Tr. catechu.............................. 200 | "
Tr. cardam comp...................... 100 | "
Mist. cretæ.....................ad... 1000 | "

M.—Dose, five c. c.

14.—Tonic Mixture.

℞   Pepsinæ .... 20 | gm.
    Quiniæ sulph .... 6 | "
    Acid. nit. muriat. dil............... 50 | c. c.
    Glycerinæ................................. 100 | "
    Aquæ ....ad... 1000 | "

M.—Dose, twenty c. c.

15.—Laxative Mixture.

℞   Magnes. sulph........................... 250 | gm.
    Ext. glycyrrhizæ...................... 100 | "
    Ext. sennæ fl........................... 50 | c. c.
    Elix. aurantii.......................... 250 | "
    Aquæ bullient..................ad... 1000 | "

M.—Dose, one hundred c. c.

16.—Diaphoretic and Diuretic.

℞   Tr. digitalis............................. 100 | c. c.
    Potass. iodid........................... 100 | gm.
    Potass. acet............................ 200 | "
    Pilocarpin. chlorid................... 1 .50 "
    Spt. æther. nit......................... 300 | c. c.
    Syr. scillæ............................... 150 | "
    Syr. simplicis..................ad... 1000 | "

M.—Dose, five c. c

17.—Diuretic.

R Potass. bicarb............................ 150 | gm.
Ext. buchu fl .... 300 | c. c.
Ext. uvæ ursi fl .... 200 | "
Tr. hyoscyami............................ 150 | "
Acaciæ pulv............ .... 50 | gm.
Olei sassaf............................. 75 | c. c.
Aquæ camph......................ad... 1000 | "

M.—Dose, five c. c.

18.—Gonorrheal Mixture.

R Copaibæ bals............................ 200 | c. c.
Liq. potassæ............................ 50 | "
Spt. æther nit .... 300 | "
Spt. lavand. comp...................... 150 | "
Syr. simplicis...................ad... 1000 | "

M.—Dose, five c. c.

19.—Gonorrheal Mixture.

R Gurjun bals............................ 300 | c. c.
Liq. potassæ........................... 50 | "
Tr. cardam. comp....................... 200 | "
Syr. simplicis..................ad... 1000 | "

M.—Dose, five c. c.

20.—Tonic.

R Tr. ferri chlorid...................... 200 | c. c.
Tr. cantharidis........................ 100 | "
Elix. aurantii......................... 400 | "
Aquæ........................ad... 1000 | "

. M.—Dose, five c. c.

21.

℞	Zinci. sulph...................................	I	gm.
	Cupri sulph...................................		30 "
	Acid. tannici...............................	I	.50 "
	Spt. lavand. comp.....................	100	c c.
	Aquæ...............................ad...	1000	"

M.—Injection.

22.

℞	Acid. carbol. cryst......................	20	gm.
	Zinci sulph................................	4	"
	Glycerinæ................................	50	c. c.
	Olei cinnamomi........................	2	"
	Aquæ..............................ad...	1000	"

M.—Injection.

23.

℞	Ext. hydrast. fl...........................	100	c. c.
	Olei eucalypti............................	100	"
	Mucil. acaciæ............................	250	"
	Aquæ.............................ad...	1000	"

M.—Injection.

25.—Tonic.

℞	Ferri et potass. tart.....................	6	gm.
	Acid. salicylici...........................		.30 "
	Tr. calumbæ.............................	200	c. c.
	Syr. simplicis............................	200	"
	Aquæ bullient...................ad...	1000	"

M.—Dose, five c. c.

26.—Tonic.

R   Quiniæ sulph......................... 40 | gm.
Tr. ferri chlorid......................... 200 | c. c.
Spt. chloroformi......................... 1 |.50 "
Glycerinæ................................. 250 | "
Aquæ........................ad... 1000 | "
M.—Dose, five c. c.

27.—Tonic.

R   Cinchonæ sulph......................... 20 | gm.
Tr. ferri chlorid......................... 100 | c. c.
Spt. chloroformi......................... 150 | "
Elix. aurantii......................... 200 | "
Aquæ........................ad... 1000 | "
M.—Dose, c. c.

8.—Anti-Periodic.

R   Quiniæ sulph......................... 80 | gm.
Acid. sulph. arom......................... 200 | c. c.
Tr. capsici......................... 50 | "
Syr. rhei. arom......................... 500 | "
Glycerinæ ....ad... 1000 | "
M.—Dose, five c. c.

30.—Tonic.

R   Acid. nit. muriat. dil......................... 200 | c.c.
Tr. calumbæ......................... 200 | "
Tr. cardam. comp......................... 200 | "
Glycerinæ......................... 200 | "
Aquæ........................ad... 1000 | "
M.—Dose, five c. c.

31.

℞ Chloral. hydrat........................... 200 | gm.
    Camphoræ................................. 200 | "
    Tr. aconit. rad.......................... 200 | c. c.
    Tr. opii................................. ?00 | "
    Olei. menth. pip......................... 10 | '
    Alcoholis.........................ad... 1000 | '

M.—External use.

32.

℞ Chloroformi.............................. 300 | c. c.
    Tr. aconit. rad.......................... 50 | "
    Liq. ammoniæ............................ 200 | "
    Olei. olivæ............................. 300 | "
    Alcoholis ....ad... 1000 | "

M.—External use.

33.

℞ Chloroformi.............................. 100 | c. c.
    Tr. aconit. rad.......................... 50 | "
    Spt. camphoræ........................... 50 | '
    Liniment. saponis....................... 500 | '
    Alcoholis........................ad... 1000 | '

M.—External use.

34.

℞ Peruviani bals........................... 300 | c. c.
    Tr. myrrhæ.............................. 300 | "
    Benzoini comp ....ad... 1000 | "

M.—External use.

35.

℞ Ammoniæ chlorid....................... 10 | gm.
Alcóholis................................ 300 | c. c.
Aquæ .... 1000 | "
M.—External use.

36.

℞ Tr. arnicæ............................. 250 | c. c.
Liniment. saponis...................... 250 | "
Alcoholis...........................ad... 1000 | "
M.—External use.

37.

℞ Iodinii .... 15 | gm.
Chloroformi............................ 100 | c. c.
M.—External use.

38.

℞ Potass. chlorat....................... 50 | gm.
Acid. tannici.......................... 30 | "
Glycerinæ.............................. 250 | c. c.
Aquæ..............................ad... 1000 | "
M.—Gargle.

39.

℞ Acid. tannici......................... 30 | gm.
Glycerinæ.............................. 250 | c. c.
Aquæ...........................ad... 1000 | "
M.—Gargle.

40.

℞ Acid. boracici........................... 150 | gm.
   Ung. petrolei........................... 85c | "
   M.—External use.

41.

℞ Acid. carbol. cryst...................... 50 | gm.
   Ung. petrolei........................... 950 | "
   M.—External use.

42.

℞ Ung. hydrarg. nit....................... 100 | gm.
   Acid. tannici........................... 100 | "
   Ext. hyoscyami.......................... 100 | "
   Ung. petrolei........................... 700 | "
   M.—External use.

43.

℞ Ung. hydrarg. nit....................... 200 | gm.
   Ung. petrolei........................... 800 | "
   M.—External use.

44.

℞ Iodofórmi............................... 20 | gm.
   Bals. Peruviani......................... 100 | "
   Ung. petrolei........................... 880 | "
   M.—External use.

45.

R Zinci oxidi................................ 100 | gm.
Acid. oleici............................. 900 | "
M.—External use.

46.

R Hydrarg. ammoniat..................... 100 | gm.
Tr. benzoin. comp...................... 50 | c. c.
Ung. petrolei............................ 850 | gm.
M.—External use.

47.

R Acid. crysophanici..................... 20 | gm.
Ung. petrolei............................ 980 | "
M.—External use.

48.

R Bismuthi subnit....................... 500 | gm.
Sodii bicarb............................ 500 | "
M.—Dose, one gram.

49.

R Magnesii sulph......................... 250 | gm.
"   carb........................... 250 | "
Sulphuris............................... 250 | "
Glycyrrhizæ pulv....................... 250 | "
M.—Dose, one gram.

50.

R   Zinci oxidi............................. 500 | gm.
      Iodoformi .... 500 | "
      M.—External use.

51.

R   Acid. boracici........................ 500 | gm.
      Acid. tannici .... 500 | "
      M.—External use.

52.—Tertiary Syphilis.

R   Iodinii resublim...................... 4 | gm.
      Potass. iodid........................ 80 | "
      Syr. sarsap. comp................ad... 1000 | c. c.
      M.—Dose, five c. c.

53.—Tonic.

R   Quiniæ sulph....................... 13 | gm.
      Tr. ferri. chlorid.................... ˙66 | c. c.
      Strichniæ sulph..................... | 20 gm.
      Aquæ.......................ad... 1000 | c. c.
      M.—Dose, five c. c.

54.—Syphilitic Mixture.

R   Potass. iodid....................... 120 | gm.
      Ammon muriat...................... 50 | "
      Aquæ.......................ad... 1000 | c. c.
      M.—Dose, five c. c.

55.—Syphilitic and Tonic.

℞ Hydrarg. bichlorid...................... 1 ⎫ gm.
   Ammon sesq. chlorid.................. 1 ⎪ "
   Quiniæ sulph............................. 10 ⎪ "
   Aquæ............................. .ad... 1000 ⎭ "

M.—Dose, five c. c.

56.

℞ Zinci sulph....:.. .... 6 ⎫ gm.
   Morphiæ sulph.......................... . 3 ⎪ "
   Aquæ.......................... ....ad... 1000 ⎭ c. c.

M.—Injection.

58.—Tonic.

℞ Tr. ferri chlorid........................... 20 ⎫ c. c.
   Liq. potass. arsen...................... 12 ⎪ "
   Quiniæ sulph............................. 4 ⎭ gm.

M.—Dose, one c. c.

59.—Cough Mixture.

℞ Glycyrrhizæ pulv...................... 30 ⎫ gm.
   Sacchari alb............................. 30 ⎪ "
   Acaciæ pulv............................. 30 ⎪ "
   Tr. opii camph.......................... 120 ⎪ c. c.
   Vin. antimonii.......................... 60 ⎪ "
   Spt. æther. nit.......................... 30 ⎪ "
   Aquæ.......................... ......ad... 1000 ⎭ "

M.—Dose, 20 c. c.

60.—Catarrh Snuff.

℞ Bismuthi subnit............................	8	gm.
Sacchar: alb. pulv........................	16	"
Camphoræ pulv............................	2	"
Olei gaultheriæ...........................	0	03 c.c.

M.—Use as a snuff.

COOK COUNTY HOSPITAL,

(CHICAGO, ILL.)

W. J. McGARIGLE—WARDEN.

———

CHICAGO, April 20, 1885.

DR. C. F. TAYLOR.

Yours at hand. We have but few established formulæ in use here, the hospital having assumed such dimensions as to demand a drug room in each ward. The following are those in use at present:

———

Mist. Ammon. Murias.

℞ Ammon. mur.............................. ℥ vj
    Morphiæ sulph.......................... grs. xij
    Antimon. et pot. tart................... grs. viij
    Syr. glycyrrhizæ........................ ℥ xvj
    M.

———

Hydrocyanic Acid Cough Mixture.

℞ Acidi hydrocyanici dil................. ℨ j
    Syr. scillæ..............................
    Syr. ipecac.......................āā... ℥ i
    Syr. tolutani....................ad... ℥ viij
    M.

Liniment.

℞ Aquæ ammon............................   ℥ iv
   Tr. camphoræ............................
   Tr. arnicæ...........................āā...   ℥ iv
   Alcoholis..................................   ℥ xl
   Aquæ......................................   O iv
   M.

Alterative.

℞ Iod. potass...............................   ℨ viij
   Iodinii.......................................   grs. viij
   Syr. sarsap...............................   ℥ viij
   M.

Very respectfully yours,

F. P. MURPHY, Druggist.

MASSACHUSETTS
GENERAL HOSPITAL.
(BOSTON.)

BOSTON, March 3, 1885.

DR. C. F. TAYLOR.

Dear Sir:—In reply to yours of the 24th inst. would say, we have no printed formulary, but have a number of prescriptions which are peculiar to the Massachusetts General Hospital, and only used by the hospital staff. I will give you the R's that I consider peculiar to the hospital, and if I can give you any further information would be very glad to do so.

Yours very truly,

WM. L. A. CAMERON,

For the Sup't.   Apothecary.

Hospital Pills.

R   Ex. colocynth comp.................... grs. iij
      Pulv. rhei............................... gr. j
      Nucis vomicæ.......................... gr. ¼

M.—Ft. pil. No. j.

4 4 44

4 44 44 4

4 444

4 44444444444444444444

Hospital Diarrhœa Mixture.

℞ Tr. cinnamomi.........................
Tr. opii.................................
Tr. catechu.....................āā... p. e.
M.—Dose, ℥ ss.

Hospital Solution Salts.

℞ Magnes. sulph........................ ℥ ij
Aq. menth. pip........................
Aquæ.............................āā... ℥ ss
M.—Dose, ℥ iv.

Hospital Cough Mixture.

℞ Morph. sulph................. .... gr. j
Syr. simp............................. ℥ iv
Chloroformi .... ♏ ʌv
M.—Dose, ℥ j.

Hospital Fever Mixture.

℞ Spt. æth. nit ....
Spt. chloroformi.....................
Liq. ammon acet...............āā... p. e.
M.—Dose, ℥ j every hour.

Shaw's Specific.

℞ Iod. potass................................ grs. v
Hydrarg. biniod....................... gr. 1-12
Aquæ.................................
Syr. zingib.................. ......āā... ℥ ss
M·—Dose, ℥ j, three times daily.

MARYLAND WOMAN'S HOSPITAL.

(BALTIMORE, MD.)

House Tonic.

℞   Tr. ferri. chlor..............................   ℥ iij
     Quiniæ sulph..............................   ℥ iv gr. **xvj**
     Strychinæ sulph...........................   grs. viij
     Aquæ ....   O ij

M.—Filter.   Sig.   One teaspoonful three times a day after meals.

House Injection.

℞   Zinci sulph...............................   ℥ iv
     Acidi carbolici...........................   ℥ ij
     Aquæ.....................................   O ij

M —One ounce to a pint of water   Use as a vaginal injection; from one to three syringefuls from two to four times a day.

These are the only established formulæ.   Each case is treated according to indications presented.

ST. JOHN'S HOSPITAL.

(BROOKLYN, N. Y.)

ST. JOHN'S HOSPITAL,
BROOKLYN, N. Y., April 27, 1885.

DR. TAYLOR,

Dear Doctor :—You was here a short time since and wanted me to give you a few prescriptions which we have used with advantage in the hospital. The following are such :

General Sedative Cough Mixture.

℞ Morphiæ sulph............................ grs. iv
Acidi hydrocyanici diluti............. fl. ℥ ij
Syrupi tolutan........................... fl. ℥ viij

M.—Sig. Teaspoonful as needed.

Diarrhœa Mixture.

℞ Tr. catechu.............................
Tr. opii camph..................āā... fl ℥ j
Misturæ cretæ........................... fl ℥ ij

M.—Sig. One or two teaspoonfuls as needed.

In Cystitis.

℞ Fl. ext. buchu comp.....................
Tr. conii.......................āā... f. ℥ j ss
M.—Sig. One teaspoonful three times a day.

Another.

℞ Acidi benzoici........................... grs. lxx)
Sodæ bi-boras........................... ℥ ij
Aquæ menth. pip....................... fl ℥ v.
M.—Sig. Tablespoonful three times a day.

A Tonic Pill to be Used in Chronic Constipation.

℞ Ext. nucis vom.........................
" belladonnæ.................āā... grs. v
" aloes soc........................... grs. x
Quiniæ sulph.............................
Ferri sulph. exsic....................āā... grs. xx

M.—Make into twenty pills. Sig. One three times a day

I may send you more at another time.
Very respectfully,
Resident Physician.

ST. LOUIS CITY HOSPITAL.

(ST. LOUIS, MO.)

OFFICE OF SUPERINTENDENT OF CITY HOSPITAL,
ST. LOUIS, March 22, 1885.

C. F. TAYLOR, M. D.,
Philadelphia, Pa.

Dear Sir:—Your letter of the 18th inst. received. We have no printed formulary, and our established formulary is only for antiseptics after Lister, Nussbaum, etc., which, of course, everyone has. We prepare our own gauze from caleramic cloth, using, however, iodoform dry dressings for wounds, abscesses and the like. I use five per cent. carbolized boiled linseed oil for burns and frost-bites, leaving them exposed to the air without further dressings. We use boric acid solutions in washing cavities after aspirating, where we do not have to resort to free opening. In the latter resort, we commonly employ two and a half or five per cent. solutions of carbolic acid. Corrosive sublimate solution, one part to a thousand, we use on occasion. I use the metric system in prescribing—have done so for six years—and every dose given to our nearly seven thousand patients a year is prescribed especially; *i. e.*, a small bottle or quantity at a time. We have no standard mixtures or prescriptions, but vary according to indications. Cinchonidine has been used exclusively instead of quinine for the past nine years with the best results, and not in large doses at that. To mention some particular way more often used in giving a particular remedy, like equal parts of salicylic acid and acetate of potash in syrup of lemon, is too elementary and didactic.

Yours truly,

D. V. DEAN.

Supt. and Surgeon in charge.

CINCINNATI HOSPITAL.

(CINCINNATI, OHIO.)

———

CINCINNATI, O., March 20, 1885.

DR. C. F. TAYLOR,

Editor *Medical World.*

Dear Sir :—Yours of the 18th, addressed to the superintendent of this hospital, has been referred by him to me, for answer. The Cincinnati Hospital has no printed formulary, and does not use one.

Our list of drugs and chemicals include *everything* that is used by the regular schools of medicine.

The hospital is conducted on a very liberal plan, and all new remedies are given a fair and thorough test as soon as they are obtainable; and, if found really valuable, their use is continued. Many remedies are in constant use in the hospital which are as yet comparatively unknown outside.

Very few actual prescriptions, as that word is commonly understood, are written. There is kept in every ward a large, portable medicine case which contains all the remedies in general use in that ward, the medicines being kept in the form of solutions, powders or pills, most convenient for administration. The resident physicians in making their rounds prescribe simply the required number of grains, or drachms, etc., of the medicine, and 'hey are obtained from this stock.

New prescriptions are only written when some new remedy is desired, or certain combinations which cannot be made up from the ward supply. The ward supply is replenished daily from the druggist's department, and is frequently overhauled by him.

In the same way every ward is supplied with all the instruments in ordinary use in that ward.

The subject of treatment is a very large one, and I take it, you want only a general answer. The hospital staff, as a rule, believe in very little medication.

In the treatment of continued fevers, we make large use of external cold, either in the form of sponging, ice caps, cold baths, the wet pack, or ice-water coils.

Quinia is used extensively, but most of the stronger preparations, as kairin, are no longer used, being considered too depressing and dangerous.

In most diseases the principal object in the treatment is to build up and sustain the strength of the patient until the affection has run its course.

The surgeons use very extensively iodoform, powdered boracic acid, mercury bichloride solution, and in less amount, carbolic acid.

Dr. E. W. Walker is probably entitled to priority in the use of boracic acid powder for the treatment of compound fractures.

Fractures are dressed almost entirely by plaster of Paris applications, either modified Bavarian, or made of plaster rollers.

For fracture of the femur, Dr. D. S. Young has a very excellent, yet simple device of his own, which makes extension by the use of weights, and supports the entire limb in a shallow box, so that the thigh can be examined in its entirety, without any movement or pain.

The anæsthetics used are ether and the a. c. e. mixture. The muriate of cocaine is used as a local anæsthetic by the oculists and gynæcologists.

Yours etc.,

FRANK W. HENDLEY, M. D.,

Senior Resident Physician, Cincinnati Hospital.

WESTERN
PENNSYLVANIA HOSPITAL
FOR THE INSANE.

(DIXMONT, PA.)

———

DIXMONT, ALLEGHANY Co., PA., March 21, 1885.

DR. C. F. TAYLOR:

DEAR DOCTOR: In answer to your letter I may say that we have no regular form of medicines here, in fact we give very little. Many of our patients are broken down physically as well as mentally, and we depend on tonics, etc., to build them up and return them to health of body and mind.

We use almost no sleeping medicine, no chloral nor hyoscyamin, and only lupulin when really necessary, and little or no restraint.

Yours very truly,

H. A. HUTCHINSON,
Medical Superintendent.

U. S. NAVAL HOSPITAL.

(WASHINGTON, D. C.)

———

U. S. NAVAL HOSPITAL,
WASHINGTON, D. C., April 28, 1885.

C. F. TAYLOR, M. D.,
　Editor *Medical World,*
　Dear Doctor :—I was in Philadelphia when yours, of 18th, arrived, and I gret not having seen you to explain in person that we have no printed formulary for use in the medical corps, and that I discourage set prescriptions for routine treatment in this hospital. Careful nursing and sanitation constitute a very great part of our Naval Hospital treatment.

The sick sailor, after a warm bath, clean clothes, and rest in a comfortable bed, often requires but little else. We feed the men well and dose them as little as possible. chronic pulmonary phthisis and venereal affections constitute the larger number of our patients, and they receive the customary medical treatment.

Faithfully yours,
ALBERT L. GIHON,
Medical Director, U. S. N., in charge.

U. S. MARINE HOSPITAL.

(SAN FRANCISCO, CAL.)

— —

U. S. MARINE HOSPITAL,
SAN FRANCISCO, Cal., May 14, 1885.
C. F. TAYLOR, M. D.
Editor *Medical World*,
Philadelphia, Pa.

Dear Sir:—In reply to your letter of 18th March last requesting formulæ etc. used in this hospital, I have to say that each medical officer uses his own formulæ and varies them to suit the cases under treatment.

Very respectfully, etc.,

JNO. VANSANT,

Surg. M. H. S., in charge Hospital.

HOME OF INEBRIATES.

(SAN FRANCISCO, CAL.)

––––

SAN FRANCISCO, Cal., March 20, 1885.

C. F. TAYLOR, M. D.

My Dear Sir :—In reply to yours of the 13th inst., I have to say, we have no printed formulary in this hospital. Each case is treated separately and distinctly, and entirely on its merits. We do not use alcohol in any form. We do use milk, *the very best*, Jersey dairy, extensively, in treatment of alcoholic cases.

To procure sleep, we use bromide potassium and chloral hydrate.

℞ Potass. bromidi..............................
Chloral hydratis..................āā...   ℥ j
Aquæ.......................................   O j

M.—Sig. Of this mixture, one to two ounces every four hours until sleep is procured. If one ounce is enough, well and good; but we use two ounces if necessity require.

This does not often fail us, but when it does, we combine with each dose a drachm of tinct. hyoscyamus; or we give a hypodermic injection of morphia, say gr. ¼, and repeat in two hours if necessary. The principal thing is to overcome nervous action, and procure sleep. Immediately afterwards, we produce evacuations from the bowels and look well to the bladder. To support the patient we use milk, beef tea and soup; and to stimulate, we use acetate of ammonia in full doses. Each patient is seen twice daily, at 9 A. M. and 6 P. M., and as much oftener as necessary. If he shows a tendency to sink, the battery is used freely, and long continued.

The food is of the most nourishing character. An excellent library, cards, chess, checkers, backgammon, dominoes and pictures in great profusion are used to take the patient's mind off his disease, and with very good effect.

Yours Truly,

J. G. JEWELL,

Resident Physician and Superintendent.

N. E. cor. Stockton and Chestnut streets.

——o——

SAN FRANCISCO, Cal., March 20, 1885.

C. F. TAYLOR, M. D.,

Editor *Medical World*,

Philadelphia, Pa.

Dear Sir :—I received yours of the 13th inst. and also the copy of the chart "The Urine in Disease," for which please accept my thanks.

Dr. Alers and myself have given up our Sanitarium for Alcoholism and Opium Habit, as we found it would not answer without some *law* enforcing *restraint*, which is wanting in this State. While under my charge (as resident physician) the formulæ used were the usual combinations of chloral hydrate and potassium bromide, given were tried with success.

The opium cases (as a general rule) were treated by a
gradual reduction of the accustomed drug, combined with
tonics and nerve stimulants. I treated successfully one
case in which *one drachm* of morphia sulph. was taken
daily. This is the largest quantity, that has *actually come
under my personal observation*.

I am sorry that I cannot give you any more information
on these interesting topics.

With many thanks for your kind letter, I remain,

Yours truly,

A. P. HAYNE, M. D.

533 Kearney St.

PHARMACOPŒIA

OF THE

GERMANTOWN HOSPITAL

AND

DISPENSARY.

In prescribing the Physician will write

    1st. The patient's *record number* or *name*,

    2d. The *number* of the prescription and its *title*,

    3d. The *directions* for using,

    4th. The *date*, and

    5th. His own *signature*; thus,—

For..................................

℞ No. 4. Liquor Potassii Iodidi........... f℥ iij

  Sig.—One teaspoonful in water, three times a day.

Date.   *Signature.*

NOTE :—The arrangement of the following formulæ aims to designate the dose of each drug, and the amount required in making up a "*stock mixture*" contain in two pints.

                                 S. LEWIS ZIEGLER, M. D.

    Germantown,   *Senior Resident Physician,*

        Philada., Pa.   Germantown Hospital.

MEDICINES

FOR

INTERNAL ADMINISTRATION.

NOTE:—The doses of the following formulæ are arranged for *adults* only.

Three fluid ounces (f ℥ iij) should be dispensed when the dose is one fluid drachm (f ʒ j), and six fluid ounces (f ℥ vj) when the dose is half a fluid ounce (f ℥ ss).

LIQUORES.

1.—Liquor Quiniæ Sulphatis.

℞ Quiniæ sulphatis................ ℥ ij ʒ v ϶ j
Acid. hydrochloric. dil............ f ℥ iij
Aquæ...................q. s..ad O ij

M.—f ʒ j contains gr. v.

2.—Liquor Cinchoniæ Sulphatis.

℞ Cinchoniæ sulphatis..... .... ℥ ij ʒ v ϶ j
Acid. hydrochloric. dil........... f ℥ iij
Aquæ...................q. s..ad O ij

M.—f ʒ j contains gr. v.

3.—Liquor Sodii Salicylatis.

℞ Sodii salicylatis................ ℥ ij ʒ v ϶ j
Aquæ...................q. s..ad O ij

M.—f ʒ j contains gr. v.

4.—Liquor Potassii Iodidi.

℞ Potassii iodidi .... ℥ ij ℨ v ℈ j
Aquæ cinnamomi.........q. s..ad O ij

M.—f ℨ j contains gr. v.

5.—Liquor Potassii Bromidi.

℞ Potassii bromidi................. ℥ ij ℨ v ℈ j
Aquæ...................q. s..ad O ij

M.—f ℨ j contains gr. v.

6.—Liquor Chloralis Hydratis.

℞ Chloralis hydratis .... ℥ ij ℨ v ℈ j
Syr. acaciæ.................... O j
Aquæ..................q. s..ad O ij

M.—f ℨ j contains gr. v.

7.—Liquor Ammonii Carbonatis.

℞ Ammonii carbonatis............ ℥ ij ℨ v ℈ j
Syr. acaciæ .... O j
Aquæ..................q. s..ad O ij

M.—f ℨ j contains gr. v.

8.—Liquor Sodii Bicarbonatis.

℞ Sodii bicarbonatis............... ℥ ij ℨ v ℈ j
Aquæ.................q. s..ad O ij

M.—f ℨ j contains gr. v.

9.—Liquor Morphiæ Sulphatis.

℞ Morphiæ sulphatis............... gr. xxxij
   Aquæ........................... O ij

M.—f ʒ j contains gr. ⅛

———o———

MISTURÆ.

10.—Mistura Pectoralis.   A.

	1 Dose.	64 Doses. (Two pints.)
℞ Syr. scillæ............		
Syr. ipecac...... āā..	ℳ x	āā f ʒ j f ʒ ij ℳ xl
Spts. æther. nit.........	f ʒ ss	f ʒ iv
Liq. ammon. acetat.....		
	q. s..ad f ʒ ss	q. s. ad O ij

M.—Dose, f ʒ ss, every three or four hours.

11.—Mistura Pectoralis.   B.

	1 Dose.	256 Doses. (Two pints.)
℞ Ammonii chloridi.........	gr. v	ʒ ij ʒ v ϶ j
Syr. scillæ......	ℳ x	f ʒ v f ʒ ij ℳxl
Mist. glycyrrhizæ comp.....		
	q. s..ad f ʒ j	q. s. ad O ij

M.—Dose, f ʒ j, every three or four hours.

12.—Mistura Pectoralis. C.

	1 Dose.	128 Doses. (Two pints.)
℞ Morphiæ sulph............	gr. $\frac{1}{12}$	gr. x
Tr. hyoscyami...........	℥ xx	f ℥ x f ℥ v ℥ xx
Spts. æther. comp.........		
Syr. pruni virg.......āā..	f ℥ ss	āā f ℥ viij
Aquæ..........q. s..ad	f ℥ ij	q. s. ad O ij

M.—Dose, f ℥ j–ij, every three or four hours.

13.—Mistura Pectoralis. D.

	1 Dose.	256 Doses. (Two pints.)
℞ Morphiæ sulph..........	gr $\frac{1}{16}$	gr. xvi.
Acid. sulph. aromat......	℥ v	f ℥ ij f ℥ v ℥ xx
Tr. hyoscyami...........	℥ x	f ℥ v f ℥ ij ℥ xl
Syr. pruni virg....q. s..ad	f ℥ j	q. s. ad O ij

M.—Dose, f ℥ j, every two, three or four hours *pro re nata*.

14.—Mistura Pectoralis. E.

	1 Dose.	128 Doses. (Two pints.)
℞ Acid. hydrocyanic. dil....	℥ iij	f ℥ vj ℥ xxiv
Spts. chloroformi........	℥ x	f ℥ ij f ℥ v ℥ xx
Acid. hydrobromic. (34 %)	℥ xv	f ℥ iv
Syr. scillæ..............	℥ xx	f ℥ v f ℥ ij ℥ xl
Syr. tolutani............	f ℥ ss	f ℥ viij
Aquæ..........q s..ad	f ℥ ij	q. s. ad O ij

M.—Dose, f ℥ j–ij, every three or four hours.

15.—Mistura Cretæ Comp.

	1 Dose.	64 Doses. (Two pints.)
℞ Tr. catechu comp........		
Tr. opii camph... ..āā..	f ʒ j	āā f ʒ viij
Misturæ cretæ....q. s..ad	f ℥ ss	q. s. ad O ij

M.—Dose, f ʒ j–iv, every two or three hours.

16.—Mistura Bismuthi et Chloroformi Comp.

	1 Dose.	128 Doses. (Two pints.)
℞ Bismuthi subnitrat....		
Cretæ preparat. ..āā..	gr. x	āā ℥ ij ʒ v Ə j
Spts. chloroformi......	♏ v	f ℥ j f ʒ ij ♏ xl
Tr. opii camph........		
Tr. catechu comp.āā..	f ʒ ss	āā f ℥ viij
Misturæ cretæ...q. s..ad	f ʒ ij	q. s. ad O ij

M.—Dose, f ʒ ij, every three hours.

17.—Mistura Anti-Colica.

	1 Dose.	256 Doses. (Two pints.)
℞ Tr. opii.............		
Tr. rhei.........āā..	♏ v	āā f ℥ ij f ʒ v ♏ xx
Spts. menthæ pip......		
Spts. camphoræ...āā..	♏ v	āā f ℥ ij f ʒ v ♏ xx
Spts. chloroformi......		
Tr. capsici......āā..	♏ ij	āā f ℥ j ♏ xxxij
Tr. catechu comp.....	♏ xv	f ℥ viij
Glycerini......q. s..ad	f ʒ j	q. s. ad O ij

M.—Dose, f ʒ j, every two or three hours.

18.—Mistura Acida Astringens.

	1 Dose.	64 Doses. (Two pints.)
℞ Acid. sulph. aromat....	♏ v	f ʒ v ♏ xx
Ext. haematoxyli......	gr. x	ʒ j ʒ ij Э ij
Tr. opii camph........	f ʒ ss	f ℥ iv
Syr. zingiberis........	f ʒ j	f ℥ viij
Aquæ menthæ pip.....		
	q. s...ad f ℥ ss	q. s ad O ij

M.—Dose, f ℥ ss, every three or four hours.

19.—Mistura Creasoti Comp.

	1 Dose.	64 Doses. (Two pints.)
℞ Sodii bicarb.........	gr. x	ʒ j ʒ ij Э ij
Aquæ creasoti........		
Tr. cardamom. comp. āā	f ʒ j	āā f ℥ viij
Glycerini...........	f ʒ ss	f ℥ iv
Aquæ cinnamomi,.....		
	q. s...ad f ℥ ss	q. s. ad O ij

M.—Dose, f ℥ ss, one hour after each meal.

20.—Mistura Antacida.

	1 Dose.	64 Doses. (Two pints)
℞ Liquor. calcis........	f ʒ iij	O j ss
Aquæ menth. pip......		
	q. s...ad f ℥ ss	q. s. ad O ij

M.—Dose, f ʒ j–iv, p. r. n.

21.—Mistura Sodii et Ammonii.

	1 Dose.	64 Doses. (Two pints)
℞ Sodii bicarb..........	gr. x	℥ j ℨ ij Ә ij
Spts. ammon. aromat...	♏ xx	f ℥ ij f ℨ v ♏ xx
Syr. zingiberis........	f ℨ ss	f ℥ iv
Aquæ menth. pip.......		
q. s...ad	f ℥ ss	q. s. ad O ij

M.—Dose, f ℥ ss, three or four times a day.

22.—Mistura Sodii et Gentianæ.

	1 Dose.	64 Doses. (Two pints.)
℞ Sodii bicarb..........	gr. x	℥ j ℨ ij Ә ij
Tr. gentian. comp.....	f ℨ j	f ℥ viij
Glycerini............	f ℨ ss	f ℥ iv
Aquæ cinnamomi		
q. s..ad	f ℥ ss	q. s. ad O ij

M.—Dose, f ℥ ss, three or four times a day.

23.—Mistura Pepsini Comp.

	1 Dose.	64 Doses. (Two pints.)
℞ Strychniæ sulph.......	gr. $\frac{1}{32}$	gr. viij
Quiniæ sulph.........	gr. ij	ℨ ij gr. viij
Misturæ ferri (No. 26.).	f ℨ j	f ℥ viij
Listerini............	f ℨ ss	f ℥ iv
Liquor. pepsini.......		
q. s..ad	f ℥ ss	q. s. ad O ij

M.—Dose, f ℥ ss, before or after each meal.

24.—Mistura Pepsini et Bismuthi.

	1 Dose.	64 Doses. (Two pints.)
℞ Bismuthi subnit........	gr. x	℥ j ℨ ij Ə ij
Liquor. pepsini........	f ʒ ij	O j
Syr. zingiberis........	f ʒ ss	f ℥ iv
Aquæ menth. pip......		
q. s..ad	f ℥ ss	q. s. ad O ij

M.—Dose, f ℥ ss, immediately after each meal.

25.—Mistura Anti-Emetica.

	1 Dose.	64 Doses. (Two pints.)
℞ Acid. hydrocyanic. dil.	♏ ij	f ʒ ij ♏ viij
Spts. chloroformi	♏ v	f ʒ v ♏ xx
Aquæ creasoti........	f ʒ ij	O j
Tr. cardamom. comp..	f ʒ j	f ℥ viij
Listerini.............	f ʒ ss	f ℥ iv
Glycerini......q. s..ad	f ℥ ss	q. s. ad O ij

M.—Dose, f ℥ ss, p. r. n.

26.—Mistura Ferri.

	1 Dose.	128 Doses. (Two pints.)
℞ Tr. ferri chlor........	♏ xv	f ℥ iv
Acid. phosphoric. dil...		
Syr. limonis......āā..	f ʒ ss	āā f ℥ viij
Aquæ........ q. s..ad	f ʒ ij	q. s. ad O ij

M.—Dose, f ʒ ij, well diluted, after each meal.

27.—Mistura Ferri Aperiens.

	1 Dose.	64 Doses. (Two pints.)
℞ Ferri sulph. puræ.....	gr. j	ʒ j gr. iv
Magnesii sulph........	ʒ j	℥ viij
Acid. sulph. aromat....	ℳ x	f ℥ j f ʒ ij ℳ xl
Tr. gentian. comp.....	f ʒ j	f ℥ viij
Glycerini	f ʒ ss	f ℥ iv
Aquæ.........q. s..ad	f ℥ ss	q. s. ad O ij

M.—Dose, f ℥ ss, three or four times a day.

28.—Mistura Ferri et Ammonii Acetatis.

("Basham's Mixture.")

	1 Dose.	64 Doses. (Two pints.)
℞ Tr. ferri chlor........	ℳ vj	f ʒ vj ℳ xxiv
Acid. acetic. dil.......	ℳ vijss	f ℥ j
Liq. ammon. acetat. ...f	ʒ j	f ℥ viij
Elix. aurantii.........		
Syr. simplicis. ....āā..f	ʒ ss	āā f ℥ iv
Alcoholis	ℳ xv	f ℥ ij
Aquæ... ....q. s..ad f	℥ ss	q. s. ad O ij

M.—Dose, f ℥ ss, p. r. n.

29.—Mistura Ferri et Ammonii Citratis.

	1 Dose.	128 Doses. (Two pints.)
℞ Ferri et ammon. citrat..	gr. v	℥ j ʒ ij Ꝺ ij
Tr. gentian. comp.....		
Spts. lavandulæ comp.āā	f ʒ ss	āā f ℥ viij
Glycerini	ℳ xlv	f ℥ xij
Aquæ cinnamomi, q. s.ad	f ʒ ij	q. s. ad O ij

M.—Dose, f ʒ ij, three times a day.

30.—Mistura Arsenii et Cinchonæ.

	1 Dose.	256 Doses. (Two pints.)
℞ Liq. potass. arsenit	ℳ iv	f ℥ ij f ʒ j ℳ iv
Tr. cinchonæ comp....		
q. s..ad	f ʒ j	q. s. ad O ij

M.—Dose, f ʒ j, three times a day.

31.—Mistura Cinchonæ Comp.

	1 Dose.	256 Doses. (Two pints.)
℞ Tr. capsici............	ℳ v	f ℥ ij f ʒ v ℳ xx
Tr. nucis vom	ℳ xx	f ℥ x f ʒ v ℳ xx
Tr. cinchonæ comp....		
q. s..ad f ʒ j		q. s. ad O ij

M.—Dose, f ʒ j, diluted, three times a day.

32.—Mistura Chloridorum Comp.

("Mixture of the Four Chlorides.")

	1 Dose.	128 Doses. (Two pints.)
℞ Hydrarg. bichlor......	gr. $\frac{1}{32}$	gr. iv
Liq. arsen. chlor......	ℳ v	f ℥ j f ʒ ij ℳ xl
Acid. hydrochlor. dil...	ℳ x	f ℥ ij f ʒ v ℳ xx
Tr. ferri chlor........	ℳ xv	f ℥ iv
Syr. zingiberis........	f ʒ ss	f ℥ viij
Aquæ........ q. s..ad f ʒ ij		q. s. ad O ij

M.—Dose, f ʒ ij, well diluted, three times a day.
(Should not be administered for longer than two weeks at a time.)

33.—Mistura Hydrarg. Comp.

	1 Dose.	256 Doses. (Two pints.)
℞ Hydrarg. bichlor.	gr. $\frac{1}{32}$	gr. viij
Potass. iodidi	gr. x	℥ v ʒ ij Ə ij
Syr. sarsap. comp	f ʒ ss	O j
Aquæ......q. s..ad	f ʒ j	q. s. ad O ij

M.—Dose, f ʒ j, three times a day.

34.—Mistura Anti-Rheumatica. A.

	1 Dose.	256 Doses. (Two pints.)
℞ Potassii iodidi	gr. v	℥ ij ʒ v Ə j
Sodii salicylat.	gr. xv	℥ viij
Ext. xanthoxyli fl.		
Spts. ammon. aromat. āā	ℳ x	āā f ℥ v f ʒ ij ℳ xl
Syr. zingiberis	ℳ xv	f ℥ viij
Aquæ cinnamomi,		
q. s..ad	f ʒ j	q. s. ad Oij

M.—Dose, f ʒ j, every three or four hours.

35.—Mistura Anti-Rheumatica. B.

	1 Dose.	128 Doses. (Two pints.)
℞ Potassii nitratis		
Potassii iodidi ....āā..	gr. v	āā ʒ j ʒ ij Ə ij
Ext. cimicifugæ fl.	ℳ xv	f ℥ iv
Ol. gaultheriæ	ℳ iv	f ℥ j ℳ xxxij
Mist. guaiaci comp. (No. 36.)	f ʒ j	O j
Aquæ cinnamomi, q.s.ad	f ʒ ij	q. s. ad O ij

M.—Dose, f ʒ ij, every three or four hours.

36.—Mistura Guaiaci Comp.

		1 Dose.	256 Doses. (Two pints.)
℞	Pulv. guaiaci resinæ ...	gr. v	℥ ij ℥ v ℈ j
	Liquor. potassæ.......	ℳ ij	f ℥ j ℳ xxxij
	Sacchari albæ........	℥ j	lbs. ij
	Aquæ..(f ℥ ss) q. s..ad	f ℥ j	(O j) q. s. ad O ij

M. et ft. syrupus.—Dose, f ℥ j, every three or four hours.

37.—Mistura Anti-Pyretica.

		1 Dose.	128 Doses. (Two pints.)
℞	Antipyrini..........	gr. xx	℥ v ℥ ij ℈ ij
	Quiniæ sulph........	gr. v	℥ j ℥ ij ℈ ij
	Acid. hydrochlor. dil..	ℳ vijss	f ℥ ij
	Listerini.............	f ℥ ss	f ℥ viij
	Glycerini	ℳ xv	f ℥ iv
	Aquæ........q. s..ad	f ℥ ij	q. s. ad O ij

M.—Dose, f ℥ j–ij, p. r. n.
(To avoid any depressing effects give spts. ammon. aromat., (f ℥ ss), a half hour before administering the Antipyrine.)

38.—Mistura Anti-Febrilis. A.

		1 Dose.	64 Doses. (Two pints.)
℞	Morphiæ acetat.......	gr. $\frac{1}{12}$	gr. v
	Tr. aconit. rad........	ℳ ij	f ℥ ij ℳ viij
	Spts. æther. nit.......		
	Syr. limonis......āā..	f ℥ j	āā f ℥ viij
	Liq. ammon. acetat....		
	q. s..ad	f ℥ ss	q. s. ad O ij

M.—Dose, f ℥ ss, every three or four hours.

39.—Mistura Anti-Febrilis. B.

		1 Dose.	64 Doses. (Two pints.)
℞	Morphiæ acetat.......	gr. $\frac{1}{12}$	gr. v
	Sacchar. albæ.........	gr. x	℥ j ℨ ij Ə ij
	Spts. æther. nit........		
	Aq. camphoræ....āā..	f ℨ j	f ℥ viij
	Liq. ammon. acetat....		
	q. s..ad	f ℥ ss	q. s. ad O ij

M.—Dose, f ℥ ss, every three or four hours.

40.—Mistura Anti-Febrilis. C.

		1 Dose.	64 Doses. (Two pints.)
℞	Sodii bromidi	gr. v	ℨ v Ə j
	Tr. aconit. rad........	♏ ij	f ℨ ij ♏ viij
	Liq. potassii citrat......		
	q. s..ad	f ℥ ss	q. s. ad O ij

M.—Dose, f ℥ ss, every three or four hours.

41.—Mistura Diuretica.

		1 Dose.	128 Doses. (Two pnts.)
℞	Potassii nitrat...... .	gr. v	℥ j ℨ ij Ə ij
	Potassii acetat........	gr. x	℥ ij ℨ v Ə j
	Spts. æther. nit........	♏ xv	f ℥ iv
	Liq. ammon. acetat....	f ℨ j	O j
	Syr. limonis ...q. s..ad	f ℨ ij	q. s. ad O ij

M.—Dose, f ℨ ij, every two, three or four hours.

42.—Mistura Digitalis. A.

	1 Dose.	256 Doses. (Two pints.)
R Tr. digitalis..........	♏ v	f ℥ ij f ʒ v ♏ xx
Potassii acetat	gr. xv	℥ viij
Spts. æther. nit. q. s...ad	f ʒ j	q. s. ad O ij

M.—Dose, f ʒ j, every three or four hours.

43.—Mistura Digitalis. B.

	1 Dose.	32 Doses. (Two pints.)
R Tr. digitalis..........	♏ x	f ʒ v ♏ xx
Potassii acetat........	gr. x	ʒ v gr. xx
Infus. buchu...q. s...ad	f ℥ j	q. s. ad O ij

M.—Dose, f ℥ j, every two or three hours.

44.—Mistura Potassii Citratis.

	1 Dose.	64 Doses. (Two pints.)
R Potassii citrat........	gr. xx	℥ ij ʒ v ϶ j
Syr. ipecac..........	♏ xlv	f ℥ vj
Succi limonis..........	f ʒ jss	f ℥ xij
Aquæ.........q. s...ad	f ℥ ss	q. s. ad O ij

M.—Dose, f ℥ ss, every two hours.
(Dr. H. C. Wood's abortive treatment for bronchitis.)

45.—Mistura Juniperi et Digitalis.

	1 Dose.	32 Doses. (Two pints.)
R Potassii bitart........	gr. xxx	℥ ij
Infus. juniperi........	f ℥ ss	O j
Infus. digitalis..q.s..ad	f ℥ j	q. s. ad O ij

M.—Dose, f ℥ ss–j, every two or three hours.
(Known as the "Philadelphia treatment for dropsy.")

46.—Mistura Juniperi Comp.

	1 Dose.	64 Doses. (Two pints.)
℞ Potassii citrat.........		
Potassii bitart.....āā..	gr. x	āā ℥ j ℨ ij Ә ij
Spts. juniperi comp....	f ℨ j	f ℥ viij
Liq. ammon. acetat....		
q. s..ad	f ℥ ss	q. s. ad O ij

M.—Dose, f ℥ ss, every two or three hours.

47.—Mistura Buchu Comp.

	1 Dose.	32 Doses. (Two pints.)
℞ Foliæ buchu..........	gr. xv	℥ j
Tritici repentis........	gr. xxx	℥ ij
Potassii acetat........	gr. v	℥ ij Ә ij
Acaciæ gran..........	gr. xv	℥ j
Aquæ bullientis, q. s..ad	f ℥ j	q. s. ad O ij

M. Filtra.—Dose, f ℥ j, every one, two or three hours.

48.—Mistura Potassii Bicarb.

	1 Dose.	32 Doses. (Two pints.)
℞ Potassii bicarb........	gr. v	℥ ij Ә ij
Spts. æther. nit........	f ℨ ss	f ℥ ij
Infus. lini. ....q. s..ad	f ℥ j	q. s. ad O ij

M.—Dose, f ℥ j, every hour or two.

49.—Mistura Copaibæ Comp.

("Lafayette Mixture.")

	1 Dose.	64 Doses. (Two pints.)
℞ Balsam. copaibæ......		
Liquor. potassæ...āā..	℞ xv	āā f ℥ ij
Spts. æther. nit.......		
Spts. lavandul. comp.āā	f ℥ ss	āā f ℥ iv
Syr. acaciæ..........	f ℥ ij	O j
Aq. cinnamomi..q.s..ad	f ℥ ss	q. s. ad O ij

M.—Dose, f ℥ ss, three or four times a day.

50.—Mistura Ol. Morrhuæ Comp.

	1 Dose.	64 Doses. (Two pints.)
℞ Olei morrhuae.......	f ℥ ij	O j
Syr. calcii lacto-phosphat.	f ℥ j	f ℥ viij
Liq. calcis ....q. s..ad	f ℥ ss	q. s. ad O ij

M.—Dose, f ℥ j–iv, three times a day.

51.—Mistura Ol. Morrhuæ et Iodoformi.

	1 Dose.	128 Doses. (Two pints.)
℞ Iodoformi...........	gr ij	℥ iv gr. xvj
Ol. amygdal. amar....	℞ ¼	℞ xxxij
Emuls. ol. morrhuae,...		
q. s..ad	f ℥ ij	q. s. ad Oij

M.—Dose, f ℥ j–ij, three times a day.

52.—Mistura Hypophosphit. Comp.

	1 Dose.	256 Doses. (Two pints.)
℞ Calcii hypophos.......		
Potassii hypophos		
Sodii hypophos...āā..gr.	j	āā ʒ iv gr. xvj
Quiniæ hypophos......		
Manganesii hypo..āā..gr.	$\frac{1}{4}$	āā ʒ j gr. iv
Ferri hypophos........gr.	$\frac{1}{2}$	ʒ ij gr. viij
Strychniae hypophos...gr.	$\frac{1}{120}$	gr. ij
Liq. acid. hypophos. (50%)		
Glyc erini........āā..	♏ vi	āā f ʒ iij f ʒ jss
Aquae.........q. s..ad f ʒ	j	q. s. ad O ij

M.—Dose, f ʒ j, diluted, before or after each meal.

53.—Mistura Cascaræ Sagra dæ.

	1 Dose.	256 Doses. (Two pints.)
℞ Ext. cascaræ sagrad. fl.	♏ xv	f ʒ viij
Tr. belladon.........	♏ ij	f ʒ j ♏ xxxij
Tr. nucis vom........	♏ x	f ʒ v f ʒ ij ♏ xl
Syr. aurantii cort...q.s..ad f ʒ j		q. s. ad O ij

M.—Dose, f ʒ j, morning and evening, or t. i. d.

54.—Mistura Emmenagoga.

("Dewee's Mixture.")

	1 Dose.	64 Doses. (Two pints.)
℞ Tr. cantharidis.......	♏ v	f ʒ v ♏ xx
Tr. ferri chlor........	♏ xv	f ʒ ij
Tr. aloes	♏ xx	f ʒ ij f ʒ v ♏ xx
Tr. guaiaci ammon....	f ʒ j	f ʒ viij
Syr. simplicis..q. s..ad f ʒ ss		q. s. ad O ij

M.—Dose, f ʒ ss, three times a day.

55.—Mistura Auri et Sodii Chlor.

	1 DOSE.	256 DOSES. (Two pints.)
℞ Auri et sodii chlor	gr. $\frac{1}{10}$	gr. xxv
Tr. ferri chlor........	♏ x	f ℥ v f ʒ ij ♏ xl
Acid. phosph. dil......	♏ xx	f ℥ x f ʒ v ♏ xx
Syr. limonis...q. s..ad	f ʒ j	q. s. ad O ij

M.—Dose, f ʒ j, diluted, three times a day.

56.—Mistura Ergotæ Comp.

	1 DOSE.	256 DOSES. (Two pints.)
℞ Ext. ergotæ fl.........	♏ xv	f ℥ viij
Tr. belladon..........	♏ ij	f ℥ j ♏ xxxij
Tr. nucis vom.........	♏ x	f ℥ v f ʒ ij ♏ xl
Syr. simplicis...q. s..ad	f ʒ j	q. s. ad O ij

M.—Dose, f ʒ j, three times a day, or p. r. n.

57.—Mistura Bromidi et Ergotæ.

	1 DOSE.	128 DOSES. (Two pints.)
℞ Potassii brom.........	gr. xxx	℥ viij
Ext. ergotæ fl........	f ʒ ss	f ℥ viij
Glycerini............	♏ xv	f ℥ iv
Syr. aurantii cort..... q. s. ad	f ʒ ij	q. s. ad O ij

M.—Dose, f ʒ j–ij, three times a day, or p. r. n.

58.—Mistura Bromidum.
("Mixed Bromides.")

	1 Dose.	64 Doses. (Two pints.)
℞ Ammonii brom........		āā ℥ j ℨ ij Э ij
Sodii brom.......āā.. gr. x		
Potassii brom......... gr. xx		℥ ij ℨ v Э j
Syr. simplicis........ f ℨ ij		O j
Aquæ cinnamomi,q. s. ad f ℥ ss		q. s. ad O ij

M.—Dose, f ℨ j–iv, p. r. n.

59.—Mistura Sedativa.

	1 Dose.	128 Doses. (Two pints.)
℞ Chloralis hydrat.......gr. x		℥ ij ℨ v Э j
Potassii brom.........gr. xv		℥ iv
Tr. cannab. indicæ.... ♏ xv		f ℥ iv
Tr. hyoscyami........ ♏ xxx		f ℥ viij
Glycerini .... ♏ xv		f ℥ iv
Syr. zingiberis...q.s..ad f ℨ ij		q. s. ad O ij

M.—Dose, f ℨ ij, p. r. n.

60.—Mistura Digitalis et Pilocarp. Comp.
("Jim Jam Mixture.")

	1 Dose.	64 Doses. (Two pints.)
℞ Tr. nucis vom........		
Tr· capsici.......āā.. ♏ xv		āā f ℥ ij
Tr. digitalis..........		
Ext. pilocarp. fl...āā.. ♏ xv		āā f ℥ ij
Ext. erythroxyli fl......		
Ext. valerianæ fl..āā.. f ℨ j		āā f ℥ viij
Syr. simplicis, q. s. ad.. f ℥ ss		q. s. ad O ij

M.—Dose, f ℥ ss, every two or three hours, or until *marked diaphoresis* appears.

APPENDIX—

SELECTIONS FROM THE NEW
HOSPITAL FORMULARY
OF THE
Department of Public Charities and Correction
OF THE
CITY OF NEW YORK.

MIXTURES FOR DISEASES OF THE RESPIRATORY ORGANS.

Cough Mixture for Adults.
(Infants' Hospital.)

℞ Ammonii chloridi............................. ʒ 1
Spir. ætheris comp........................... fl ʒ 6
Syr. pruni Virginianæ. .... fl ʒ 2
Aquæ ....q. s. ad fl ʒ 4
Dissolve and mix. Dose, a teaspoonful.

Mistura Antasthmatica.
"ASTHMA MIXTURE."
(Out-Door Practice.)

℞ Codeinæ sulphatis............................ gr. 4
Potassii iodidi .... gr. 32
Chloroformi purificati....................... ℳ 80
Syrupi.. fl ʒ 3
Mucilaginis acaciæ....................q. s. ad fl ʒ 5
Dissolve. Dose, a teaspoonful.

Dr. S. S. Burt.

Mistura Antasthmatica.

(Fothergill's.)

R Ammonii iodidi............................. gr. 120
   Ammonii bromidi........................... gr. 180
   Syr. tolutani.............................. fl ʒ 2
   Tinct. lobeliæ............................. fl ʒ 5

Dissolve and mix.   Dose, a teaspoonful.

Mistura contra Tussim.

"HOST COUGH MIXTURE."

R Tinct. hyoscyami.............................
   Tinct. opii camphoratæ......................
   Syr, scillæ.................................
   Syr. tolutani....................āā part. æqu.

Mix.   Dose, a teaspoonful.

Mistura Expectorans, "Stokes."

STOKES' EXPECTORANT.

R Ammonii carbonatis........................ gr. 32
   Extr. senegæ fl.............................
   Extr. scillæ fl........................āā.. fl ʒ 1
   Tinct. opii camphoratæ..................... fl ʒ 6
   Aquæ...................................... fl ʒ 4
   Syrupi tolutani.....................q. s. ad fl ʒ 4

Dissolve and mix.   Dose, a teaspoonful.

Mistura Expectorans, "Struma."

(Out-Door Practice.)

R Ammonii chloridi........................... gr. 45
   Syrupi ferri iodidi........................ ℳ 45
   Syrupi senegæ.............................
   Syrupi pruni virginianæ....................
   Syrupi acaciæ......................āā.. fl ʒ 1
   Olei morrhuæ.............................. fl ʒ 3

Dissolve and mix.   Dose, 1½ teaspoonfuls every 3 hours. to
a child of 4 years, in Bronchitis with Struma.

Dr. T. H. Holgate.

TONICS.

Loomis' Tonic.

℞ Quininæ sulphatis............................. gr. 15
Tr. ferri chloridi............................. fl ℥ 2
Spir. chloroformi............................. fl ℥ 3
Aquæ.. fl ℥ 1
Glycerini............................q. s. ad. fl ℥ 2
Dissolve and mix. Dose, a teaspoonful.

Mistura Ferri et Quininæ Citratis.

(Insane Asylum.)

℞ Ferri et quininæ citratis...................... ℥ 3
Tinct. nucis vomicæ......................... fl ℥ 5
Syrupi hypophosphitum...................... ℥ 8
Aquæ..............................q. s. ad fl ℥ 16
Dissolve and mix. Dose, 2 teaspoonfuls.

Mistura Ferri et Strychninæ.

(Bellevue Hospital.)

℞ Strychninæ sulphatis...................... gr. 1
Ferri et quininæ citratis.................... ℥ 3
Ferri pyrophosphatis....................... ℥ 2
Tinct. gentian comp.......................
Aquæ..............................āā.. fl ℥ 4
Dissolve and Mix. Dose, 2 teaspoonfuls.

Mistura pro Anæmia.

(Out-Door Practice.)

℞ Ammonii chloridi........................... ℥ 2
Tinct. ferri chloridi........................ fl ℥ 4
Glycerini................................. fl ℥ 1
Aquæ...............................q. s. ad fl ℥ 3
Dissolve and mix. Dose, a teaspoonful.

Dr. W. H. Katzenbach

Mistura Tonica.—"Special Tonic."
(Bellevue Hospital.)

℞ Quininæ sulphatis.............................   gr. 30
    Tinct. nucis vomicæ..........................
    Tinct. ferri chloridi.....................āā..   ℳ 160
    Acidi phosphor. dil..........................   fl ℥ 1
    Syrupi................................q. s. ad   fl ℥ 4
Dissolve and mix. Dose, a teaspoonful.

Ward Tonic.
(Bellevue Hospital.)

℞ Ferri et quininæ citr ....
    Ferri et strychninæ citr.................āā..   ℥ 2
    Infusi calumbæ...............................   fl ℥ 16
Dissolve and mix. Dose, a tablespoonful (containing nearly
1-28 grain of strychnine).

Ward Tonic.
(Fothergill's.—Charity Hospital.)

℞ Quininæ sulphatis............................   gr. 16
    Strychninæ sulphatis ....   gr.   ½
    Potassi citratis.............................   gr. 90
    Tinct. ferri chloridi.................... ..   fl ℥ 5
    Syrupi.......................................   fl ℥ 1
    Aquæ.............................q. s. ad   fl ℥ 4
Dissolve and mix. Dose, a teaspoonful.

—o—

MIXTURES FOR DISEASES OF THE DI-GESTIVE ORGANS.

Diarrhœa Mixture, "Loomis."

Tinct. lavandulæ comp........................   fl ℥ 2
Tinct. opii..................................
Tinct. rhei ....āā..   fl ℥ 4
Olei sassafras..............................   gtt. 40
Mix. Dose a fluid drachm after each movement. Should
it fail to act, add Tinct. Catechu fl ℥ 1.

Mistura Naphthalini.

NAPHTHALIN DIARRHŒA MIXTURE.

(Bellevue Hospital.)

℞ Naphthalini recryst......................... gr. 320
Tinct. capsici................................. gtt. 16
Olei menthæ pip........................... gtt. 2
Alcohol.......................................
Mucilag. acaciæ........................āā.. fl ℥ 1

Dissolve the naphthalin in the alcohol; add the tincture and oil; and lastly. mix with the mucilage Shake the mixture well before dispensing. Dose, 2 fluid drachms.

Note.—Commercial naphthalin is not pure enough for internal administration. Only the re-crystallized naphthalin should be used.

Mistura Stomachica.

(Bellevue Hospital.)

℞ Tinct. nucis vomicæ..........................
Tinct. capsici............................āā.. fl ℥ 1
Tinct. cinchon. comp.......................
Tinct. gentian. comp.................āā.... fl ℥ 1

Mix. Dose, a teaspoonful before meals.

—-o--—

MIXTURES FOR DISEASES OF THE NERVOUS SYSTEM.

"Delirium Mixture."

℞ Potassii bromidi.............................. ℥ 2
Tinct. lupulini...............................
Tinct. digitalis.........................āā.. fl ℥ 2
Tinct. valerian. ammon...................... fl ℥ 4
Aquæ.................................q. s. ad fl ℥ 2

Dissolve and mix. Dose, a teaspoonful.

Mistura Anti-epileptica.

℞ Sodii bromidi................................
   Potassii bromidi...........................
   Ammonii bromidi.....................āā..   ℨ 3
   Potassii iodidi ....
   Ammonii iodidi. ....āā..   ℨ 1½
   Ammonii carbonatis.........................   ℨ 1
   Tinct. calumbæ.......... ....   fl ℨ 1½
   Aquæ........................q. s. ad   fl ℨ 8

Dissolve and mix. Dose, 1½ fluid drachms before meals, and
3 fluid drachms at bed-time.

Dr. Brown-Sequard.

Mistura Bromata.

℞ Sodii bromidi...............................
   Ammonii bromidi....................āā..   gr. 20
   Tinct. opii.................................   ♏ 5
   Aquæ........................q. s. ad   fl ℨ 1

Dissolve and mix. One dose. In restlessness of melan-
cholia and the occasional excitement of primary and secon-
dary dementia, especially when the general physical condition
is poor.

Mistura Chloral et Hyoscyami.

℞ Chloral.......................................   gr. 15
   Extr. hyoscyami fl...........................   ♏ 12
   Aquæ........................q. s. ad   fl ℨ 1

Dissolve and mix. One dose, to be repeated as often as necessary. A double dose may be given, when required.

In maniacal excitement of general paresis and inflamma-
tory states in general, where the exhibition of hyoscyamine
alone increases the severity of the disease after its hypnotic
effect has passed off, and is, therefore, contra-indicated.

Mistura Ergotæ Composita.

℞ Extr. ergotæ fl...............................   ♏ 30
   Potassii bromidi.............................   gr. 20
   Extr. hyoscyami fl...........................   ♏ 25
   Aquæ........................q. s. ad   fl ℨ 1

Dissolve and mix. One dose, three times daily, in maniacal
excitement of chronic and recurrent mania.

Mistura Nervina.

HAMMOND'S OR VANCE'S MIXTURE.

℞ Quininæ sulphatis..........................
Ferri pyrophosphatis.....................āā..   ℥ 1
Strychninæ: ....   gr. 1
*Acidi phosphorici diluti....................   fl ℥ 2
Syrupi zingiberis.............................   fl ℥ 2
Aquæ.............................q. s. ad   fl ℥ 4

Add the pyrophosphate of iron to one fluid ounce of the water, and dissolve it by agitation. Mix the sulphate of quinine and the strychnine with the diluted phosphoric acid and the syrup of ginger. Then pour the two solutions together, and add enough water to make the product measure 4 fluid ounces.

Dose, a teaspoonful.

* For preparing mixtures like the above, a special diluted phosphoric acid should be kept in stock, prepared as follows:

Glacial Phosphoric Acid..........   gr. 600
Water............enough to make   fl ℥ 10

Mistura pro Delirio—"D. T. Mixture."

(Bellevue Hospital.)

℞ Potassii bromidi.............................   ℥ 1
Chloral.....................................   ℥ 4
Tinct. digitalis..............................
Tinct. capsici...............................
Tinct. zingiberis..... ....
Spir. ammoniæ arom.....................
Syr. aurantii cort.....................āā..   fl ℥ 1
Aquæ.............................q. s. ad   fl ℥ 8

Mistura Antineuralgica—Burt's Mixture.

(Out-Door Practice.)

℞ Potassii iodidi..............................   gr. 30
Tinct. opii.................................   ♏ 80
Ext. gelsemii fl..............................   ♏ 45
Ext. cimifugæ fl............................   ♏ 75
Syr. sarsaparillæ comp.....................   fl ℥ 6
Aquæ.............................q. s. ad   fl ℥ 2

Dissolve and mix. Dose, a tablespoonful every four hours, in muscular rheumatism and neuralgia affecting the chest.

Dr. S. S. Burt.

DIRECTIONS FOR D. T. MIXTURE.

Dissolve and mix. Dose, a tablespoonful.

MIXTURES FOR RHEUMATISM AND GOUT.

Mistura Antirheumatica (I.)

(Bellevue Hospital.)

℞ Potassii acetatis............................ ʒ 6
Vini colchici sem............................ fl ʒ 3
Aquæ ... . q. s. ad fl ʒ 4
Dissolve and mix. Dose, a teaspoonful.

Mistura Antirheumatica (II.)

(Charity Hospital.)

℞ Potassii iodidi...............................
Sodii salicylatis..........................āā.. ʒ 2
Vini colchici sem.......................... fl ʒ 2
Aquæ. ....q. s. ad fl ʒ 4
Dissolve and mix. Dose, a tablespoonful.

Mistura Colchici.

℞ Vini colchici sem........................... ♏ 15
Magnesii carbonatis........................ gr. 10
Spir. ætheris nitrosi.......................
Tinct. conii.............................āā.. ♏ 30
Aquæ menthæ vir..................q. s. ad fl ʒ 1
Mix. One dose.

Mistura Olei Gaultheriæ.

(Bellevue Hospital.)

℞ Olei gaultheriæ............................. ♏ 160
Mucilag. acaciæ............................. fl ʒ 2
Glycerini....................................
Aquæ....................................āā.. fl ʒ 1
Mix. Dose, one to two teaspoonfuls.

MIXTURES FOR VENEREAL DISEASES.

Mistura Biniodidi.

℞ Hydrargyri chloridi corr...................... gr. 1
    Potassii iodidi................................ ℨ 2
    Tinct. gentian. comp........................ ℨ 2

Dissolve and mix. Dose, a teaspoonful.

Note.—Tincture of cinchona or other liquids containing alkaloids should not be combined in a mixture with biniodide of mercury, or with iodide of potassium and bichloride of mercury, since the alkaloids may, under certain conditions, be precipitated as iodo-hydrargyrates, and the patient might possibly take the whole precipitate with the last dose.

"Mistura Bumstead."

℞ Copaibæ.. fl ℨ 4
    Tinct. ferri chloridi..........................
    Tinct. cantharidis ....āā.. fl ℨ 2
    Glycerini....................................... fl ℨ 4
    Syrupi..............................q. s. ad fl ℨ 4

Mix. Dose, a tablespoonful.

Mistura Copaibæ Composita.

℞ Copaibæ....................................... fl ℨ 6
    Potassii acetatis............................. ℨ ½
    Mucilag. acaciæ.............................
    Syrupi.....................................āā fl ℨ 4
    Aquæ.............................q. s. ad fl ℨ 4

Dissolve and mix. Dose, a tablespoonful.

Dr. S. Alexander.

"Mistura Lafayette."

℞ Copaibæ.......................................
    Spir. ætheris nitr...........................
    Tinct. lavandulæ comp................āā.. fl ℨ 4
    Liq. potassæ.................................. fl ℨ 1
    Syrupi... fl ℨ 4
    Mucilag. acaciæ...................q. s. ad fl ℨ 4

Mix. Dose, a tablespoonful.

Mistura Potassii Iodidi.
(Charity Hospital.)

℞ Potassii iodidi............................ ℨ 4
    Syr. sarsaparillæ comp......................
    Tinct. gentian. comp..................āā.. fl ℨ 1
Dissolve and mix. Dose, a tablespoonful.

——o——

DIURETIC MIXTURES.

Mistura Buchu Composita.
(Out-Door Practice.)

℞ Ext. buchu fl............................ fl ℨ 4
    Tinct. hyoscyami........................ fl ℨ 2
    Potassii acetatis........................ ℨ 1
    Syrupi ziugiberis....................... fl ℨ 1
    quæ.............................q. s. ad fl ℨ 4
    Dive and mix. Dose, a tablespoonful, in water, every
    6urs. In catarrhal cystitis.
Dr. W. B. Anderton.

Mistura Buchu et Scoparii.
"SPECIAL DIURETIC."
(Bellevue Hospital.)

℞ Potassii acetatis........................ ℨ 5
    Spir. ætheris nitrosi.................... fl ℨ 4
    Infusi digitalis......................... fl ℨ 6
    Infusi scoparii.............q. s. ad fl ℨ 16
Dissolve and mix. Dose, a tablespoonful.

Mistura Diruretica.—"A.B.C. Diuretic."
(Charity Hospital.)

℞ Potassii acetatis......................
    Potassii bicarbonatis.................
    Potassii citratis..............āā.. ℨ 1
    Infusi tritici rep........q. s. ad fl ℨ 4
Dissolve and mix. Dose, a tablespoonful.
Dr. R. Guiteras.

Mistura pro Cystitide.—"Cystitis Mixture."

(Bellevue Hospital.)

R̶ Liquoris potassæ...... ....   fl ʒ 1
    Mucilag. acaciæ.................... . ...   fl ʒ 4
    Tinct. hyoscyami....................q. s. ad   fl ʒ 2

Mix. Dose, a teaspoonful.

Mistura pro Cystitide, "Polk."

"CYSTITIS MIXTURE, POLK."

(Bellevue Hospital.)

R̶ Potassii bicarbonatis..........................   ʒ 1
    Tinct. hyoscyami............ ....   fl ʒ 1
    Infusi buchu.......................q.. s. ad   fl ʒ 6

Dissolve and mix. Dose, a tablespoonful.

Dr. W. M. Polk.

---o---

MISCELLANEOUS.

Glycerite of Gelatin.—Glue Burn Mixture.

R̶ Gelatini albi..................................   ʒ 7½
    Glycerini.......................................   fl ʒ 1
    Acidi carbolici...............................   fl ʒ 2
Aquæ...   fl ʒ 16

Soak the gelatin in the cold water until it is soft; then heat it on a water-bath until it is melted. Add the glycerin and continue heating until a firm, glossy skin begins to form on the surface of the mixture, in the intervals of stirring. Now add the carbolic acid and mix intimately.

Note.—This mixture may be kept ready prepared, and is best prepared in well-closed glass or porcelain jars. When it is wanted for use, it is heated on a water-bath until just melted, and applied with a soft, flat brush over the burned part, where it will form a strong, flexible skin.

Mistura pro Ambustis, Buck.

BUCK'S BURN MIXTURE.

℞ Tragacanthæ pulv............................   ℥ 2
   Acaciæ pulv.................................   ℥ 4
   Syrupi fusci ....
   Aquæ bullientis...........................āā..   fl ℥ 16

Mix the tragacanth and acacia with the molasses to a homogeneous paste, then add the boiling water under constant stirring.

Linimentum Anodynum—"Jacob's Oil."

(Charity Hospital.)

℞ Camphoræ......................................
   Chloral....................................āā..   ℥ 2
   Chloroformi..............................
   Ætheris fortioris..........................āā..   fl ℥ 2
   Tinct. opii ....
   Olei sas-afras............................āā..   fl ℥ 1
   Linim. saponis....................q. s. ad   fl ℥ 16

Dissolve and mix.

Oleum Ricini cum Atropina.

ATROPINE AND CASTOR OIL.

(Out-Door Practice.)

℞ Atropinæ..................................... .   gr. 2
   Olei ricini...................................   fl ℥ 1

Triturate the atropine with a little of the castor oil to a smooth paste. then gradually incorporate the remainder of the castor oil, and continue the trituration until the atropine is dissolved.

One drop to be applied to the eye every half hour. To be used in burns of the eye, by lime.

Dr. W. F. Mittendorf.

Note.—The solution of the alkaloid in the oil may be hastened by a gentle heat. The alkaloid atropine, and not the sulphate or any other salt, should be used for this preparation

Petrolatum Zinci Salicylicum.

"SALICYLIC ZINC OINTMENT."

℞ Acidi salicylici .... gr. 15
Zinci oxidi...................................
Amyli pulv.............................āā.. ʒ 2½
Petrolati.. ʒ 1
Mix.

Unguentum Fuscum—Brown Ointment.

(Charity Hospital.)

℞ Argenti nitratis............................. gr. 80
Ext. stramonii ....
Ext. belladonnæ.......................āā.. gr. 480
Ung. hydrarg. ox. rub........................
Cerati plumbi subacet...................āā.. gr. 30
Bals. peruviani...................... q. s. ad ʒ 16
Mix. To be applied to indolent ulcers.

Note.—The above mixture is chemically incompatible, and is known to be so by the physicians using it, but is reported to give satisfactory results.

Pilulæ Antirheumaticæ.

℞ Ext. colocynth. comp........................ gr. 45
Ext. colchici rad.............................. gr. 30
Ext. hyoscyami............... ....
Hydrarg. chor. mitis.....................āā.. gr. 10
Mix. Divide into thirty pills.

Note.—Ext. colchici radicis, U. S. Ph. 1880, is equivalent to *extractum colchici aceticum*, Us. Ph. 1870.

Pilulæ Colchici.

℞ Jalapæ pulv....................................
Aloes..
Hydrarg. chlor. mitis.........................
Ext. colchici rad.......................āā.. gr. 12
Ext. nucis vomicæ........................... gr. 3
Mix. Divide into twelve pills. One three times daily, or every three hours, until griping is felt.

Dr. A. L. Loomis.

Pilulæ Opii, Belladonnæ et Tiglii.

"LEAD COLIC PILL."

℞ Opii pulv.. gr. 1
    Olei tiglii.. gtt. 1
    Ext. belladonnæ............................... gr. ⅙
Mix. One pill.

Dr. A. L. Loomis.

Pilulæ Post Partum.

BARKER'S "POST PARTUM" PILLS.

℞ Extr. colocynth. comp........................ gr. 20
    Ext. aloes....................................... gr. 15
    Ext. hyoscyami............................... gr. 10
    Ext. nucis vomicæ............................ gr. 5
    Res. podophylli...............................
    Ipecacuanhæ pulv...... ....aa.. gr. 1
Mix. Divide into twelve pills.

Dr. Fordyce Barker.

Pilulæ pro Subinvolutione.

(Bellevue Hospital.)

℞ Ferri redacti..................................
    Quninæ sulphatis.......................ää.. gr. 48
    Ergotini purificati........................... gr. 24
    Strychninæ sulphatis......... .... gr. ½
    Ext. Gentianæ................................ q. s.
Mix. Divide into twenty-four pills.

Note.—The proportions of reduced iron and sulphate of
quinine are sometimes altered. "Ergotin" is a name applied,
not to an active principle, but to a purified extract of ergot, in
which a large proportion of the inert constituents have been
removed by means of alcohol.

Pulvis Acidi Borici et Iodoformi.

(Out-Door Practice.)

℞ Acidi borici.................................... gr. 180
    Acidi tannici................................... gr. 10
    Iodoformi....................................... gr. 60
Mix. To be applied, once a day, to everted and granulated
eyelids.

Dr. W. F. Mittendorf.

Pulvis Iodoformi Compositus.

(Charity Hospital.)

℞ Iodoformi.................................... part. 1
    Zinci carbonatis............................. part. 3

Mix. To be applied with a blower, or by means of a dusting box, as a dressing in venereal sores, ulcers, etc.

Pulvis Iodoformi Inodorum.

(Out-Door Practice.)

℞ Iodoformi.................................... gr. 180
    Acidi tannici................................ gr. 60

Mix. To be applied to ear, mornings and evenings, in granulations of external auditory canal.

Dr. W. F. Mittendorf.

A-C-E Mixture.

℞ Alcohol... fl ℥ 1
    Chloroformi purificati......................... fl ℥ 2
    Ætheris fortioris.............................. fl ℥ 3

Mix. For Anæstheria.

Liquor Hypophosphitum Compositus.

(Bellevue Hospital.)

℞ Calcii hypophosphitis......................... gr. 640
    Sodii hypophosphitis.......................... gr. 384
    Potassii hypophosphitis....................... gr. 128
    Liq. Ferri hypophosphitis.................... ℳ 384
    Aquæ.................... ....q. s. ad fl ℥ 32

Dissolve and filter. Dose, one to four fluid-drachms.

Dr W. M. Polk.

Note.—The solution of hypophosphite of iron is that of the New York and Brooklyn Formulary, six minims of which contain one grain of the salt.

Liquor Potassii Chloratis et Ferri.

"Jacobi's Special."

℞ Potassii chloratis............................ gr. 80
    Tinct. ferri chloridi........................ ♏ 160
    Glycerini.................................... fl ℥ 2
    Aquæ.............. :...............q. s. ad fl ℥ 8

Dissolve and mix.   Dose, half a fluid-ounce.

Dr. Abraham Jacobi.

Mistura Anodyna—"Gibson's Special."

(Bellevue Hospital.)

℞ Tinct. opii..................... .... ♏ 90
    Ext. belladonnæ fl. .... ♏ 16
    Chloroformi purificati....................... ♏ 30
    Syrupi.......................................
    Aquæ.......................................āā.. fl ℥ 4

Mix.

Morell's Embalming Liquid.

℞ Arsenious acid............................... 14 parts.
    Soda (caustic)..... .... 7 parts.
    Carbolic acid..........................a suff. quantity
    Water.......................enough to make 100 parts.

Dissolve the arsenious acid and the caustic soda in twenty parts of water with the acid of heat. Allow the solution to cool, and then add to it just enough carbolic acid to render it opalescent. Finally, add enough water to make the product weigh one hundred parts.

Used for embalming, and for preserving anatomical specimens.